TOM MACKROLA

When It's Time To Sell

A Strategic Guide for Homeowners Facing Difficult Property Decisions

HOUSE MONEY PRESS
PUBLISHING THE FUTURE

First published by House Money Press, a division of ProfitSeas Publishing 2026

Copyright © 2026 by Tom Mackrola

First edition

ISBN: 979-8-9994323-4-6

Contents

1

Introduction

The letter arrived on a Tuesday. It wasn't the first notice, there had been others, but they'd been easy to ignore. Bills. Official looking envelopes. The kind of mail you set aside and tell yourself you'll deal with "later." But this one was different. Bold text across the top: NOTICE OF FORECLOSURE SALE. A date. An auction. A timeline that suddenly made everything very, very real.

The house had been inherited eight months earlier when her mother passed away. It came with a reverse mortgage... something she didn't fully understand at the time, but assumed could be "dealt with eventually." There were unpaid property taxes. Code violations from years of deferred maintenance. And now, a foreclosure sale scheduled in six weeks.

She didn't want the house. She'd never wanted it. But she also didn't want to lose the equity, money her mother had built over decades, money that could help stabilize her own shaky financial situation if she could just figure out how to access it. The problem was, she had no idea what to do. She didn't know if she even could do anything at this point. Maybe it was too late. Maybe the house was already gone. She was stuck, overwhelmed, and running out of time.

If any part of that story sounds familiar...if you've inherited property you don't want, if you're facing foreclosure or financial pressure, if you own a rental that's draining you, or if you just have a house that no longer serves your life...this book is for you.

The Problem This Book Solves

There are millions of people who own property they don't want, can't afford, or can't manage. Some inherited it unexpectedly. Some bought it during a different chapter of their life that no longer applies. Some are facing financial hardship, divorce, health issues, or simply the reality that the property has become a burden instead of an asset.

The problem isn't just owning the property. The problem is not knowing what to do about it.

Most people facing this situation don't have a clear picture of their options. They don't know if selling makes sense, or when, or how. They don't understand the timeline pressures, the financial implications, or the strategies that could preserve equity they didn't even know they had. They feel stuck, paralyzed by complexity, overwhelmed by the process, and worried they'll make the wrong decision.

This book exists to change that.

Who This Book Is For

This book is written for anyone who owns property that's creating stress, costing money, or no longer serving their goals.

You might be: Facing foreclosure or a reverse mortgage deadline and unsure if you can still salvage equity, Inheriting property you don't want or don't know how to handle, Burned out as a landlord dealing with difficult tenants, repairs, and the stress of property management, Stuck with a property from a divorce or breakup that's tying you to a past you're ready to leave behind, An aging homeowner whose housing no longer fits your physical needs or lifestyle, Holding a property that's bleeding money every month and wondering when to cut your losses, Trying to figure out if selling makes sense, or if holding, renting, or another strategy is better

If any of these situations describe you, keep reading. This book was written with you in mind.

What This Book Is NOT

Before we go any further, let's be clear about what this book is not:

This is not a sales pitch. We're not trying to pressure you into hiring us or making a decision you're not ready for. Every chapter is designed to educate, not manipulate.

This is not a "get rich quick" real estate guide. We're not promising you'll make a fortune by following some secret formula. This book is about making smart, strategic decisions with property you already own.

This is not a one size fits all answer. Your situation is unique. We can't tell you exactly what to do...but we can give you the framework, knowledge, and tools to make the best decision for your specific circumstances.

This is not overly technical or full of jargon. Real estate can be complicated, but we've worked hard to make this book accessible, practical, and straightforward. You don't need to be an expert to understand what we're covering here.

What This Book IS

This book is an honest, comprehensive guide to understanding your options when it's time to sell property.

It's written by real estate professionals who work with distressed, inherited, and problem properties every single day. We've seen the patterns. We know what works, what doesn't, and what people wish they'd known before they made decisions.

We wrote this book because we got tired of watching people: Lose equity they didn't have to lose, Make emotional decisions they later regretted, Try to handle complex situations alone and fail, Get misled by bad advice or incomplete information, Stay stuck because they didn't know what was possible

This book gives you the information you need to make better decisions, whether you work with us, another professional, or decide to handle things yourself.

Our goal is simple: **help you make your next move your best move.**

What You'll Learn

This book is structured to take you from confusion and over-whelm to clarity and confidence.

Here's what we'll cover:

Part 1: Understanding Your Situation (Chapters 1 2) We'll help you assess your relationship with the property, recognize the signs that it's time to sell, and understand what's really happening financially and emotionally.

Part 2: Your Options (Chapters 3 4) You'll learn about the three main paths available, selling for cash, listing on the market, or holding strategically, and understand what working with professionals actually looks like.

Part 3: The Selling Process (Chapters 5 8) We'll walk you through preparing the property, using pre sale inspections strategically, listing effectively, and navigating the under contract period to closing.

Part 4: Common Mistakes and Misconceptions (Chapters 9 10) You'll learn why FSBO (For Sale By Owner) often backfires, and we'll clear up confusion about the recent NAR lawsuit and commission changes.

Part 5: Real Stories and Strategic Moves (Chapters 11 13) We'll share real case studies of sellers who faced tough situations and found successful outcomes. Then we'll dive into advanced strategies like 1031 exchanges, tax optimization, and creative solutions for complex scenarios.

Part 6: Tools and Action Steps (Chapters 14 15) You'll get practical checklists, timelines, worksheets, and reference materials to guide you through the process, plus final words of encouragement and clarity.

By the time you finish this book, you'll have: A clear understanding of whether selling makes sense for your situation, Knowledge of your options and the trade offs of each, Realistic expectations about timelines, pricing, and process, Tools to prepare and execute a successful sale, Confidence to make informed decisions and work effectively with professionals

How to Use This Book

You can read this book straight through from beginning to end, that's how it's designed to flow.

Or, if you're facing an urgent timeline or specific challenge, you can jump to the chapters most relevant to you:

Facing foreclosure or a deadline? Start with Chapter 2 (Signs It's Time to Sell) and Chapter 4 (Working With Professionals)

Trying to decide if you should sell? Begin with Chapter 1 (Understanding Your Relationship With the Property) and Chapter 3 (Your Options)

Ready to list but need guidance? Jump to Chapters 5 8 (the selling process)

Curious about advanced strategies? Go to Chapter 13 (Protecting Your Equity)

Need practical tools right now? Head to Chapter 14 (The Seller's Toolkit)

Keep Chapter 14 (The Seller's Toolkit) bookmarked. It's your quick reference section with checklists, timelines, and worksheets you'll use throughout the process.

This book is designed to be both educational and practical, something you read once for understanding, then reference again and again as you move through your own situation.

A Promise

If you commit to reading this book with an open mind and honest self assessment, here's what I promise you'll have by the end:

Clarity about your situation, your options, and what makes sense for your goals

Confidence in your ability to navigate this process and make informed decisions

Control over a situation that might have felt out of control before

You might decide to sell. You might decide to hold. You might realize your situation is more complex than you thought and needs professional guidance. Or you might discover options you didn't know existed.

Whatever you decide, it will be an informed decision, not a panicked reaction, not avoidance, not blind hope that things will somehow work out.

And that makes all the difference.

One More Thing Before We Begin

Real estate decisions are deeply personal. They're tied to money, family, identity, and sometimes painful life circumstances.

If you're feeling overwhelmed, ashamed, or frustrated about your property situation, please know: you're not alone, and this isn't a reflection of your worth or capabilities.

Life happens. Situations change. Inheritances come with complications. Relationships end. Health issues arise. Financial pressure builds.

What matters isn't how you got here. What matters is what you do next.

And right now, by picking up this book and seeking information, you're doing exactly the right thing. You're taking control. You're educating yourself. You're preparing to make the best decision you can with the information available.

That's not weakness. That's wisdom.

So take a deep breath. Turn the page. And let's figure this out together.

Your next move starts now.

2

Understanding Your Relationship With the Property

Before you can decide whether selling makes sense, you need to understand what you're actually dealing with.

Not the romanticized version. Not what the property was supposed to be. Not what it might become someday if circumstances were different.

What it actually is, right now, today, and what it's costing you to keep it.

This chapter helps you get honest about your relationship with the property. Because clarity is the foundation of good decision making.

How Did You Get This Property?

The origin story matters. How you acquired a property shapes how you think about it, what emotional weight it carries, and what options feel available to you.

9

You Bought It

Maybe you purchased this property intentionally, as a home, an investment, a rental. At the time, it made sense. It fit your life, your budget, your goals.

But circumstances change. Jobs relocate. Relationships end. Kids grow up and move out. Markets shift. What worked five years ago might not work now.

If you bought the property and now it's not serving you, that's not failure. That's life. Situations evolve, and smart decisions evolve with them.

You Inherited It

Inheriting property sounds like a gift. Sometimes it is. But often, it comes with complications you didn't choose and responsibilities you didn't ask for.

Maybe it's across the country. Maybe it's full of belongings you don't know what to do with. Maybe there's a reverse mortgage, unpaid taxes, or family disputes about what to do with it. Maybe you just don't want to be a landlord or deal with the maintenance.

Inherited property can feel like an obligation disguised as an asset. And if it's creating stress instead of value, it's worth questioning whether keeping it makes sense.

You Kept It After a Life Change

Divorce. Breakup. Death of a spouse. Relocation for work. These life transitions often leave people with property that's tied to a chapter of life that's closed.

The house you shared with someone you're no longer with. The rental property you bought together. The family home that's too big now that you're alone.

These properties carry emotional weight. And sometimes, the healthiest move is to let them go.

You Acquired It Creatively

Maybe you got the property through a foreclosure purchase, a tax sale, a contractor payoff, or some other non traditional route. You saw an opportunity, you took it, and now you're sitting on equity, but also complexity.

Creative acquisitions can be great investments. They can also be time bombs if the property comes with legal issues, title problems, or more work than you anticipated.

Do You Actually Want It?

This sounds like a simple question, but most people avoid asking it honestly.

"Want" isn't just about liking the property. It's about whether owning it aligns with your current life, goals, capacity, and priorities.

Ask yourself:

If you could start over today, knowing everything you know now, would you choose to own this property?

If the answer is no, that tells you something important.

Does this property make your life better or harder?

If it's causing stress, costing money, creating conflict, or demanding time and energy you don't have, it's making your life harder, even if it has sentimental value or theoretical future potential.

Are you keeping it because you want to, or because you don't know what else to do?

There's a difference between strategic holding and paralysis. If you're keeping the property because you're overwhelmed by the idea of selling, that's not a plan, it's avoidance.

Is This an Asset or a Liability?

The words we use matter. People call property an "asset" because, on paper, it has value. But real assets generate more than they cost. If a property drains resources, creates obligations, and provides no tangible benefit, it's not functioning as an asset, it's functioning as a liability.

Here's how to tell the difference:

Financial Test

Does the property generate income that exceeds all expenses (mortgage, taxes, insurance, maintenance, repairs)?

If yes, and the cashflow is meaningful, it's a financial asset.

If no, if you're putting money in every month, it's a financial liability.

Does the property have equity (market value minus what you owe)?

If yes, you have something to work with. If no, you're underwater, and every month you hold it risks losing more.

Are expenses rising faster than any income the property generates?

Property taxes increase. Insurance premiums climb. Repairs get more expensive as the property ages. If your costs are accelerating and income isn't, the math is working against you.

Opportunity Cost Test

What else could you do with the equity tied up in this property?

If you have $50,000 in equity locked in a property that costs you $800/month, that's not just $800/month in expenses. It's also $50,000 you can't use for anything else, down payment on better housing, debt payoff, business investment, financial cushion.

What opportunities are you missing by holding this property?

Could the equity fund something that improves your life more than this property does?

Time and Energy Test

How much mental space does this property occupy?

If you're constantly worrying about it, avoiding calls related to it, or losing sleep over it, that's a real cost, even if it doesn't show up on a spreadsheet.

How much time do you spend managing it?

Coordinating repairs, dealing with tenants, handling paperwork, driving to the property to check on things, all of this is time you're not spending on work, family, or things you actually want to do.

If someone offered to take this property off your hands for free right now, would you feel relief?

That's a telling question. If the answer is yes, the property is a burden, not an asset.

What Are the Carrying Costs?

Most people underestimate what it actually costs to own property. Let's break it down.

Monthly Obligations

Mortgage payment (principal and interest)
Property taxes (often escrowed in mortgage payment, but still a cost)
Homeowners insurance (or landlord insurance for rentals)
HOA fees (if applicable)
Utilities (if vacant or between tenants)
Property management fees (if you hire a manager for a rental)

Irregular but Inevitable Costs

Repairs and maintenance (HVAC, plumbing, roof, appliances, things break)
Landscaping and exterior upkeep
Pest control
Seasonal maintenance (gutter cleaning, snow removal, etc.)
Vacancy costs (lost rent during turnover or when you can't find a tenant)

Hidden Costs

Your time (coordinating repairs, managing tenants, handling issues)
Stress and mental energy (dealing with problems, worrying about what might break next)

Opportunity cost (what else you could do with the equity or monthly cashflow)

Add it all up honestly. What's this property actually costing you per month, per year?

Now compare that to what it's providing, income, housing, appreciation potential, peace of mind.

If the costs outweigh the benefits, you're funding a liability.

The 2 A.M. Stress Test

Here's a simple way to assess whether this property is serving you or draining you:

It's 2 a.m. You can't sleep. Your mind is racing.

What are you thinking about?

If the answer involves this property, worrying about upcoming bills, dreading a repair you can't afford, stressing about tenants or legal issues or what might go wrong next, that's not just a financial problem. That's a quality of life problem.

Properties should provide stability, security, or income. If yours is providing stress and sleepless nights instead, that's a clear signal.

What Happens If You Do Nothing?

Inaction is a decision. And sometimes, it's the most expensive decision you can make.

If you do nothing:

Deferred maintenance compounds. That small roof leak becomes structural damage. That minor plumbing issue becomes a major flood. Waiting doesn't make problems cheaper, it makes them worse.

Carrying costs continue accumulating. Every month you hold the property is another month of mortgage payments, taxes, insurance, and utilities. If you're not generating income from it, that's money disappearing.

Opportunity passes by. Market conditions change. Equity you could have captured erodes. Options that exist today might not exist six months from now.

Stress continues. The mental and emotional weight doesn't go away because you're avoiding it. It grows.

If there are legal timelines involved, foreclosure, probate, reverse mortgage deadlines, waiting can mean losing equity you could have preserved by acting sooner.

Doing nothing feels safe. But it's often the riskiest move of all.

What Are You Trying to Accomplish?

This is the most important question in this chapter, and maybe the whole book.

What do you actually want to achieve?

Not what you think you're supposed to want. Not what someone else thinks you should do. What do you want?

Do you want:

Financial relief, less stress, fewer bills, more breathing room?

Liquidity, access to equity you can use for something else?

Simplicity, fewer responsibilities, less to manage?

A fresh start, to close a chapter and move forward?

To maximize value, to get the most money possible from this property?

To resolve a family dispute or legal complication?

To stop worrying and sleep better at night?

Your answer to this question shapes everything else. Because the "right" decision for someone trying to maximize value looks different from the "right" decision for someone trying to exit quickly and reduce stress.

There's no wrong answer here. Just honest self assessment.

Moving Toward Clarity

By now, you should have a clearer picture of:

How you got this property and what emotional weight it carries

Whether you actually want to keep it

Whether it's functioning as an asset or a liability

What it's costing you in money, time, and stress

What you're trying to accomplish

This clarity is the foundation for everything that comes next. Because you can't make good decisions about what to do with a property until you're honest about what it is and what it's costing you.

In the next chapter, we'll look at the specific signs that indicate it's time to sell, the red flags, the tipping points, and the patterns that suggest holding on is doing more harm than good.

Let's keep going.

3

Signs It's Time to Sell

There's a difference between wanting to sell and needing to sell. And then there's the space in between where selling isn't urgent in the emotional sense, but strategically, it's the smartest move you could make right now.

Most people don't wake up one morning and decide to sell a property on a whim. The realization builds slowly. Small stresses accumulate. Bills stack up. A repair gets delayed. A phone call goes unanswered. And one day, you realize you're not managing a property anymore you're managing a situation that's managing you.

This chapter isn't about convincing you to sell. It's about helping you recognize when a property has shifted from being an asset that serves you to a situation that needs resolution and understanding what that actually means for your timeline and options.

If you're reading this, you're already ahead of most people. You're asking questions. You're looking for clarity. That's the first step.

Physical Signs: When the Property Itself Is Telling You Something

Properties communicate. Sometimes they whisper. Sometimes they demand attention.

Deferred maintenance is one of the clearest signals. When you start noticing that the roof has been "needing attention" for two years, or the HVAC system is limping through another season, or there's a slow leak you keep meaning to call someone about those aren't just repairs waiting to happen. They're indicators that the property needs more than you can give it right now.

This is incredibly common, especially with inherited properties or homes that have been vacant for a while. Here's what to watch for:

Repairs are piling up faster than you can address them. One thing breaks, then another, then three more. You're not keeping up you're falling behind. This happens to almost everyone who inherits a property they weren't planning for.

You're avoiding the property. If checking in on the house feels like a chore you dread, pay attention to that. Your instincts are telling you something important.

Code violations or city notices have arrived. Whether it's overgrown grass, peeling paint, or structural issues flagged by inspectors, these don't resolve themselves. They compound. And they come with deadlines.

The property is vacant and it's been vacant for a while. Empty homes deteriorate faster than occupied ones. Pipes freeze. Pests move in. Vandalism becomes a risk. Insurance gets complicated.

Major systems are aging out. Roof, furnace, water heater,

foundation concerns when multiple big ticket items are near the end of their lifespan, the math gets overwhelming fast.

If you're nodding along to several of these, the property is communicating something important: It needs attention you may not be able to provide right now.

And that's completely normal. Recognizing this isn't a failure. It's honest assessment. It's clarity. And clarity is what allows you to make better decisions.

Financial Signs: When the Numbers Tell a Story

Real estate is supposed to build wealth, not drain it. But sometimes the math shifts, and what once seemed like an asset starts costing money every month.

This is one of the most common patterns we see and one of the most misunderstood. Many people think they need to "just hold on a little longer" until things improve. But holding on costs money, and those costs accumulate faster than most people realize.

Here are the financial patterns that indicate you're in a situation that needs strategic attention:

You're putting money into the property every month just to keep it. Whether through mortgage payments, insurance, property taxes, utilities, or maintenance if money flows into the property more than it returns to you, the math is working against you.

Taxes and insurance are climbing. Property taxes don't stay flat. Insurance premiums increase, especially in certain markets or with certain property conditions. These aren't discretionary costs they're mandatory and they grow.

You can't afford the next repair. When the furnace dies and

you don't have the cash to replace it, you're one emergency away from a much larger problem. This is especially common with inherited properties where the previous owner deferred maintenance.

The mortgage balance is close to (or exceeds) the property's value. If you owe more than the home is worth, or if equity is razor thin, the property can trap you financially. Understanding this early is critical because it affects which options are available to you.

Carrying costs are competing with your other goals. That property payment isn't just a number on paper it's money that could be going toward your current living situation, retirement, starting a business, or building stability elsewhere.

You inherited the property and the financial obligations came as a surprise. This might be the most common scenario we encounter. Inheriting a home sounds like a gift and sometimes it is. But when it comes with a reverse mortgage balance, unpaid property taxes, or years of deferred maintenance, it can feel more like inheriting a problem.

The Reverse Mortgage Reality

Let's talk about this specifically because it's something many heirs don't understand until they're already in it.

When someone passes away and leaves a home with a reverse mortgage, the loan becomes due. The timeline is usually six months, though sometimes it can be extended slightly. During that time, heirs have three options:

Pay off the loan balance (refinance or pay cash)

Sell the home and use proceeds to pay off the loan

Let the home go to foreclosure

Here's what most people don't realize: if there's equity in the home, that equity belongs to the heirs. If the home is worth $200,000 and the reverse mortgage balance is $120,000, there's $80,000 of equity that can be recovered but only if the home sells before the foreclosure happens.

We see this situation regularly. Heirs receive a notice. They're overwhelmed. They don't know what their options are. They assume it's "too late" or "too complicated." Meanwhile, the clock is running.

If this is your situation right now, here's what you need to know: you likely still have options, but the timeline matters. The earlier you understand what's happening and explore your choices, the more runway you have to get a better outcome.

Emotional Signs: When the Property Costs More Than Money

Money isn't the only cost of owning property. There's an emotional cost too and for many people, it's the emotional weight that becomes unsustainable first.

Feeling dread about a property is a signal worth paying attention to. Properties shouldn't make you anxious. They shouldn't steal your sleep or create a knot in your stomach every time you think about them.

This is what emotional strain looks like, and it's more common than you might think:

You're procrastinating on decisions. Calls go unreturned. Paperwork sits unopened. You know you need to do something, but you're frozen. This often happens because the situation feels overwhelming and you're not sure where to start.

You're overwhelmed by responsibility. Maybe you inherited

the property and never wanted to be a landlord. Maybe you bought it with a partner and the relationship ended. Maybe you're just tired of being the person who has to handle everything.

Family disputes are brewing. Multiple heirs, different opinions, no clear decision maker. The property becomes the center of conflict instead of an asset everyone benefits from. This is exhausting and often prevents any action from happening.

You're tired of being the problem solver for this property. Every issue tenant problems, repairs, tax bills, violations lands on you. And you're exhausted.

You avoid thinking about the property altogether. Out of sight, out of mind works until it doesn't. Then the problem is bigger and the options are fewer.

Emotional exhaustion is a completely valid factor in decision making. You don't have to justify it. If the property is costing you peace of mind, that's real, and it matters.

Legal Signs: When Timelines Become Critical

Some property situations come with deadlines real deadlines that don't negotiate.

Foreclosure timelines are the most time sensitive. If your property has a scheduled auction date, you're working against a clock. But here's something many people don't realize until they talk to a professional: you may still have options, even close to the sale date.

Selling before the auction can preserve whatever equity remains and protect your credit. But the key word is before. Once the auction happens, those options disappear.

Why Short Sales Need Time

If you owe more on the property than it's currently worth or close to it you may be looking at what's called a short sale. This is where the bank agrees to accept less than the full loan balance to avoid foreclosure.

Short sales are complex. They require:

Written authorization from the homeowner (or heirs) allowing the real estate broker to communicate with the lender

A complete financial package submitted to the bank

Negotiation with the loss mitigation department

Bank approval, which can take weeks or months

This is why early action matters. Short sales need runway. The more time you have before the auction date, the more options exist. If you're three weeks from a sale date and just starting the process, your options narrow significantly. If you're three months out, there's much more room to work.

This isn't about creating false urgency. It's about understanding how these processes actually work so you can make informed decisions about timing.

Other Legal Timelines to Understand

Probate delays. Inherited properties stuck in probate can take months or even years to resolve. Meanwhile, the property sits, deteriorates, and costs money. Understanding your legal standing and options during probate is critical.

Reverse mortgage deadlines. As mentioned earlier, these loans become due when the owner passes away. Six months is standard, though extensions are sometimes possible. The sooner you understand what's required, the better.

Divorce or partnership dissolution. When a property is tied to a relationship that's ending, clarity about options becomes essential. Trying to co manage property post split rarely works long term.

Tax liens and encumbrances. Unpaid property taxes, mechanic's liens, or other claims against the property compound over time. These don't go away they grow. Addressing them while there's still equity means you have more options.

If any of these apply to your situation, understand this: time is a factor, but so is having the right guidance. These are complex situations that benefit from professional help. That's not a sales pitch it's just the reality of how these processes work.

Market Signs: When External Conditions Matter

Sometimes the best reason to act has nothing to do with the property itself. It's about the market environment.

Real estate markets move in cycles. There are times when sellers have the advantage, and times when buyers do. Understanding where your market is right now can inform your timing.

Market patterns to be aware of:

Your neighborhood is appreciating. If property values in your area have climbed significantly, acting now locks in those gains. Markets don't climb indefinitely.

Your neighborhood is softening. If the area is trending downward businesses closing, vacancy rising, property values plateauing or declining acting sooner rather than later preserves more equity.

Interest rates affect buyer demand. When rates are low,

buyers can afford more, which often translates to stronger offers. When rates rise, buyer pools shrink.

Local development patterns are shifting. New infrastructure, businesses, or employers moving in can boost values. Conversely, major employers leaving or nearby deterioration can impact your property's value.

Market timing isn't about trying to hit the absolute peak. It's about recognizing when conditions create opportunity and being willing to act when the window is open.

The Assessment: Understanding Your Situation

Here's a simple way to assess where you stand. Go through this list honestly. These aren't "you must sell" indicators they're signals that your situation may benefit from professional guidance.

Check any that apply:

Repairs are piling up and I can't keep pace

I'm putting money into the property every month

The property has been vacant for more than six months

I inherited the property and don't want it

There's a foreclosure sale date scheduled

I'm dealing with a reverse mortgage deadline

Property taxes or insurance have increased significantly

Thinking about this property creates stress or dread

There's family conflict over what to do with it

I can't afford the next major repair

The property is stuck in probate

I'm avoiding calls or mail related to it

I feel stuck or overwhelmed by this property

The market in my area is currently strong

This property is blocking other financial goals

If you checked several of these, you're not being indecisive. You're being honest. And honest assessment is the foundation of making better decisions.

Why Understanding These Patterns Matters

The reason we're walking through all of these signs isn't to create pressure. It's to create clarity.

Most people facing these situations don't have a property problem they have an information problem. They don't know what their options are. They don't know how the timelines work. They don't know what's possible.

And when you don't know what's possible, it's easy to do nothing. Or to do the wrong thing at the wrong time.

Here's what we see happen when people understand their situation clearly:

They make better decisions. Not rushed decisions informed ones. They understand the trade offs. They know what they're working with.

They preserve more equity. Acting with clarity and appropriate timing means more options are available. More options means better outcomes.

They reduce stress. Clarity is calming. Even when the situation is complex, understanding it reduces the psychological weight.

They don't try to handle complex situations alone. Properties with foreclosure timelines, reverse mortgages, short sale potential, probate issues, or significant deferred maintenance aren't simple DIY projects. They benefit from professional guidance. That's not because you're incapable it's because these situations have moving parts, deadlines, and processes that professionals deal with every day.

What Comes Next

You've made it through this chapter, which means you're willing to look at your situation honestly. That matters.

The next question is natural: Okay, I understand what's happening. Now what are my actual options?

That's exactly what the next chapter covers. Because once you have clarity about where you are, the next step is understanding where you can go and how to get there in a way that protects your interests and creates the best possible outcome.

Let's explore those options together.

4

Your Options: Cash vs Listing vs Holding

If you made it through Chapter 2 and recognized yourself in some of those patterns, you're probably asking: Okay, so what do I actually do?

Good question. And here's the thing most people don't realize: you have more options than you think.

Even if you're facing a foreclosure deadline. Even if the property needs work. Even if you inherited something you never wanted. Even if you're overwhelmed and don't know where to start.

You have options.

This chapter breaks down the three main paths available to you, what each one looks like in practice, and how to think about which one might make the most sense for your specific situation.

There's no "one size fits all" answer here. The right choice depends on your timeline, your goals, the property's condition, and what you're trying to accomplish next. Our job is to help you understand what each path actually involves so you can make an informed decision.

Let's walk through them.

Option 1: Sell for Cash (Off Market to an Investor)

This is the fastest path from "I own this property" to "I have cash in hand and I'm done."

How It Works

When you sell to a cash buyer or investor:

The property is evaluated as is. No repairs needed. No cleaning required. No staging, no photos, no showings. The property gets assessed in its current condition.

You receive a cash offer, usually within days. This isn't a "we'll get back to you eventually" process. Cash buyers move fast because they buy with cash, no financing contingencies, no appraisal requirements, no bank approvals.

Closing happens quickly, typically 7 to 14 days. Sometimes faster if the timeline demands it. Once you accept the offer, the process moves directly to closing. No waiting for buyer financing. No lengthy contingency periods.

You walk away with a check. The transaction is complete. The property is no longer your responsibility.

When This Makes Sense

Cash sales aren't for everyone, but they're the right move in specific situations:

You're facing a foreclosure deadline. If there's a sale date on the calendar and time is short, a cash buyer may be your best (or only) option to preserve equity.

The property needs significant repairs. If the roof needs replacement, the HVAC is shot, there's foundation damage, or the property has been neglected for years, a cash buyer takes it as is. You don't spend money you don't have on repairs.

You inherited a property you don't want. Maybe it's across the country. Maybe it's filled with belongings you don't have time to sort through. Maybe you just want it resolved quickly. Cash sale solves this cleanly.

The property is vacant and deteriorating. Empty homes cost money every month and decline in condition. A fast cash sale stops the bleeding.

You need certainty and speed over maximum price. Cash transactions close. There's no buyer financing falling through at the last minute. No inspection renegotiations. No appraisal surprises. It's straightforward.

You're in a short sale situation. While short sales are complex, having a cash buyer can sometimes streamline the process with the bank because there's no financing contingency to complicate things.

What You're Trading

Here's what you need to understand: cash buyers pay less than retail market value. That's the trade off.

Why? Because they're taking on risk and responsibility you're avoiding. They're buying a property that may need $30,000 in repairs. They're dealing with the timeline pressure. They're handling the complexity. And they're doing it for profit.

So if your property might sell for $180,000 on the open market in perfect condition, a cash offer might come in at

$120,000 to $140,000, depending on what repairs are needed and current market conditions.

The question isn't "Is this fair?" The question is: "Does this solve my problem better than the alternatives?"

If you're three weeks from foreclosure and the property needs $40,000 in work, a cash offer of $130,000 that closes in 10 days might save you from losing everything. That's not a bad deal, it's the right deal for that situation.

The Real Benefit: Speed and Certainty

The biggest advantage of a cash sale isn't the price, it's the timeline and the guarantee.

You know what you're getting. You know when you're getting it. You know it's going to close. There are no surprises, no contingencies, no waiting on banks or buyers or appraisers.

For people in time sensitive situations or facing properties they simply want resolved, that certainty is worth more than squeezing out every last dollar of theoretical value.

Option 2: List the Property (For Maximum Value)

This is the traditional path: put the property on the market, let buyers compete, and sell for the highest price you can get.

How It Works

When you list a property with a real estate agent:

The property is evaluated and priced for market. An experienced agent will analyze recent comparable sales, assess your property's condition, and recommend a pricing strategy that attracts serious buyers.

The property is prepared for market. This might involve cleaning, minor repairs, staging, and professional photography. The goal is to present the property in its best possible light.

It's listed publicly on the MLS (Multiple Listing Service), Zillow, Realtor.com, and other platforms where buyers and their agents are actively searching.

Showings and open houses happen. Interested buyers tour the property. Their agents provide feedback. The market tells you what it thinks about your price.

Offers come in (assuming the property is priced correctly and marketed well). You evaluate them, negotiate terms, and accept the strongest offer.

The buyer goes under contract, which typically involves: A home inspection (where the buyer can ask for repairs or credits) * An appraisal (if they're financing the purchase) * Final loan approval from their lender, A title search and closing preparation

You close in 30 to 60 days on average, though timelines vary depending on the buyer's financing and any issues that arise during inspections or appraisal.

When This Makes Sense

Listing your property makes sense when:

You have time. If you're not facing an immediate deadline, you have the luxury of letting the market work.

The property is in decent condition (or you're willing to invest in getting it there). Buyers expect properties to show well. If yours does, you'll attract more offers and higher prices.

You want to maximize your equity. Listing on the open market typically generates the highest sale price because you're exposing the property to the largest pool of buyers.

Market conditions favor sellers. If inventory is low and demand is high, listing can create competition among buyers, sometimes even resulting in multiple offers over asking price.

You can manage the process. Listing requires coordination, scheduling showings, keeping the property accessible, responding to offers, negotiating inspection requests. If you're able to handle that (or have an agent who handles it for you), it's worth it.

What This Path Requires

Listing isn't passive. It requires some level of preparation and involvement.

Preparation costs: You may need to invest in cleaning, minor repairs, landscaping, or cosmetic updates to make the property competitive. (We'll cover what's worth doing and what's not in Chapter 5.)

Time investment: Showings happen on buyers' schedules, not yours. If the property is occupied, this can be disruptive. If it's vacant, you'll need to manage access, utilities, and security.

Emotional patience: Not every showing results in an offer. Not every offer is a good one. The process can take weeks or even months in slower markets.

Inspection and appraisal risk: Even after you accept an offer, the deal isn't done. Buyers can renegotiate based on inspection findings. Appraisals can come in low, forcing price adjustments or killing the deal entirely.

But here's the upside: when it works, it works well. You get more money. You attract buyers who see the potential in your property. You leverage market competition to your advantage.

The Real Benefit: Maximum Return

If your goal is to walk away with the most money possible, listing is typically the path to get there.

Yes, it takes longer. Yes, it involves more moving parts. But for properties that are in reasonable condition and where time isn't the enemy, the extra equity you preserve can be significant.

The difference between a $140,000 cash offer and a $180,000 retail sale is $40,000. After commissions and closing costs, you might net an extra $20,000 to $25,000. For many people, that's worth the extra time and effort.

Option 3: Hold the Property

Sometimes the best move is to not sell at all, at least not yet.

When Holding Makes Sense

There are legitimate reasons to hold onto a property:

It's cashflow positive. If you have a rental property that's generating more income than it costs to maintain, and you're comfortable being a landlord, holding can build long term wealth.

The market is temporarily down. If your area is in a short term slump but long term trends are strong, waiting out the downturn might make sense.

You're planning to move back. If you relocated for work

temporarily or for family reasons, and there's a realistic plan to return, holding might be strategic.

You have the resources and capacity. If you can afford the carrying costs, handle maintenance, and aren't stressed by the responsibility, holding is viable.

Tax or estate planning considerations. Sometimes holding makes sense for capital gains timing, estate planning, or other financial strategy reasons.

When Holding Becomes a Problem

But holding can also be a trap. Here's when it stops making sense:

You're losing money every month. If the property costs more than it generates, you're funding a liability, not holding an asset.

Deferred maintenance is piling up. Holding a property that's deteriorating doesn't preserve value, it destroys it.

You don't actually want to be a landlord. Tenant issues, repairs, middle of the night emergencies, if this isn't something you want to manage, holding a rental property will drain you.

The property is vacant. Holding an empty property is expensive and risky. It generates no income, costs money monthly, and declines in condition.

You're holding because you're avoiding a decision. This is the most common trap. People hold properties not because it makes strategic sense, but because they don't know what else to do. That's not a plan, it's paralysis.

The Hidden Cost: Opportunity Cost

Here's what most people don't calculate: what holding is costing you in missed opportunities.

If you have $50,000 in equity trapped in a property that's costing you $800/month to carry, that's not just $800/month in expenses. It's also $50,000 you can't use for anything else.

That money could be: A down payment on a property you actually want to live in, An investment in a better performing asset, A business opportunity, A financial cushion that reduces stress, Debt payoff that improves your monthly cashflow elsewhere

Holding makes sense when it serves a purpose. It stops making sense when it's just delaying a decision that needs to be made.

The Real Question: What Are You Actually Trying to Accomplish?

Here's the framework that matters most:

If your priority is speed and certainty Cash sale is probably your best path.

If your priority is maximizing equity Listing is probably your best path.

If your priority is long term wealth building and you have capacity Holding might make sense.

But notice the word "probably." Every situation has nuance.

You might need speed and want to maximize value. (In that case, we'd look at whether strategic repairs and a quick listing timeline could work.)

You might be in short sale territory where a cash buyer

simplifies bank negotiations, but maybe there's enough equity that listing still makes sense if you have a few months.

You might think you want to hold the property, but when you calculate the true carrying costs and opportunity cost, selling becomes the obvious move.

This is why professional guidance matters. These aren't simple decisions with one size fits all answers. They're strategic decisions that benefit from experience, market knowledge, and understanding how all the moving parts fit together.

Decision Framework: How to Think About Your Situation

Here's a simple way to evaluate which path might fit:

Ask Yourself These Questions:

Timeline: * Do I have a foreclosure date or other hard deadline? * Am I in a rush, or can I afford to wait 30 60 days (or longer)?

Property Condition: * Is the property in good shape, or does it need significant work? * Am I willing and able to invest in repairs/prep?

Financial Goals: * Do I need certainty of outcome, or am I willing to take some risk for potentially higher return? * What's more valuable to me: speed or maximum dollar amount?

Capacity: * Can I handle the logistics of listing (showings, open houses, negotiations)? * Do I have the emotional bandwidth for a 30 60 day process?

Long Term Strategy: * Does this property fit into my broader financial plan? * What do I want to do next after this property is resolved?

You Don't Have to Decide Alone

Here's the reality: most people facing these decisions aren't real estate professionals. They don't know how to run comps, assess repair costs, calculate net proceeds, evaluate buyer offers, or navigate short sales.

That's not a weakness, it's just reality. These are complex situations with financial, legal, and logistical components. They benefit from professional input.

The goal of this chapter isn't to tell you which path to choose. It's to help you understand what each path actually involves so that when you sit down with someone who handles these situations every day, you can have an informed conversation about what makes sense for you.

Because the right move isn't the same for everyone. It depends on your situation, your timeline, your goals, and your capacity. But the wrong move is almost always the same: doing nothing because you don't know what your options are.

Now you know what your options are.

The next chapter will walk you through what working with the right team actually looks like, what to expect, how the process flows, and what kind of guidance makes the difference between a stressful transaction and a smooth one.

Let's keep going.

5

What Working With a Professional Team Looks Like

By now you understand the signs that it might be time to sell, and you've got a general sense of your options: cash sale, listing on the market, or holding the property.

The next question is natural: What does working with someone actually look like? What should I expect?

This chapter walks you through the actual process, both paths, so you know what to expect, what questions will be asked, and how professionals evaluate your situation to recommend the best strategy.

Because here's the thing: a good real estate professional isn't trying to force you into one path or another. They're trying to understand your situation well enough to show you which option makes the most sense for your specific circumstances.

Let's break down how that happens.

The Initial Conversation: Understanding Your Situation

Whether you're exploring a cash sale or considering listing your property, the process starts the same way: with questions.

A good agent or investor partner needs to understand:

About the property:

How did you acquire it? (Purchase, inheritance, divorce, etc.)
Is it occupied, vacant, or rented?
What's the general condition? Are there known issues?
Are there any liens, back taxes, or legal complications?
What's the mortgage situation? (Paid off, current, behind, reverse mortgage, etc.)

About your timeline:

Are you facing a foreclosure date or other deadline?
How quickly do you need this resolved?
Can you wait 30 60 days, or do you need certainty in 7 14 days?

About your goals:

What are you trying to accomplish?
Is speed most important, or maximizing the sale price?
What do you plan to do after the property sells?
Are there family members or other stakeholders involved?

About your capacity:

Can you handle repairs or property prep?
Are you able to manage showings and the listing process?
Do you have funds available for pre sale improvements if needed?

These aren't interrogation questions, they're diagnostic questions. Just like a doctor can't recommend treatment without understanding symptoms, a real estate professional can't recommend a strategy without understanding your situation.

This initial conversation usually happens by phone or in person, and it takes 15 30 minutes. At the end, you should have a clearer picture of which direction makes sense: investor network or listing on the market.

Path 1: The Investor Network Evaluation

If your situation points toward a cash sale, maybe you're facing a deadline, the property needs significant work, or you just want speed and certainty, here's what the process looks like.

Step 1: Property Assessment

An investor or their representative will want to see the property. This can happen quickly, sometimes within 24 48 hours of your initial conversation.

They're evaluating: Overall condition (structure, systems, cosmetics) * Repair needs and estimated costs, Neighborhood and comparable sales, Timeline and any legal complications

This isn't a formal inspection, it's a walkthrough to understand what they're working with.

Step 2: The Cash Offer

Based on that assessment, you'll receive a cash offer. This typically happens within a few days.

Here's what you need to understand about cash offers:

Cash buyers are evaluating the property based on: 1. What it will cost them to acquire it (purchase price) 2. What it will cost them to repair/renovate it 3. What they can sell it for after repairs (or rent it for if holding) 4. Their profit margin for taking on the risk and work

The offer will be below retail market value. This is not negotiable in principle, it's how the math works. If your property might sell for $180,000 in perfect condition on the open market, but it needs $35,000 in repairs, a cash offer might come in around $120,000 to $135,000.

That difference accounts for: The repair costs they'll incur, The time and project management required, The risk they're taking (unexpected issues, market shifts) * Their profit for doing this as a business

The question isn't "Is this fair?" The question is: "Does this solve my problem better than the alternatives?"

If you're three weeks from foreclosure, have no funds for repairs, and need certainty, a $130,000 cash offer that closes in 10 days might be exactly the right solution, even if the property could theoretically sell for more under different circumstances.

Step 3: The Timeline

If you accept the cash offer, the timeline is straightforward:

Day 1 3: Title work begins, contract is signed

Day 7 10: Any remaining due diligence is completed

Day 10 14: Closing happens, you receive funds

Sometimes it's even faster if the situation demands it. Cash buyers don't need mortgage approval, appraisals, or lengthy contingency periods. They're buying as is with cash, so the process is streamlined.

Why Off Market Investors Are Different

Here's something important to understand: not all investor buyers are the same.

Off market investors the ones who work through established networks and buy directly from sellers, are typically experienced, professional buyers. They: Purchase multiple properties per year (sometimes dozens) * Have financing ready (cash or proven hard money sources) * Close reliably because it's their business, Know how to evaluate properties quickly and accurately, Rarely back out once under contract

These are serial buyers with systems, experience, and credibility.

On market investors the ones who find properties listed on the MLS, are more variable. Some are experienced, but many are: Buying their first or second property ever, Still learning how to evaluate deals, More likely to get nervous during inspections, More prone to aggressive renegotiation or backing out, Less reliable because they're less experienced

If you list your property and an investor makes an offer through the MLS, you might still get a good outcome, but the reliability factor is different. The buyer might be solid, or they might flake after tying up your property for three weeks.

Off market networks filter for proven, reliable buyers. That consistency matters when you're dealing with tight timelines or stressful situations.

Path 2: The Listing Appointment Process

If your situation points toward listing the property, you have time, the property is in reasonable condition, and you want to maximize value, here's what that process looks like.

Step 1: The Listing Appointment

This is a sit down meeting (in person or virtual) where the agent walks you through:

Market Analysis: * Recent comparable sales in your area, Current active listings (your competition) * Market trends and buyer demand, Days on market for similar properties

Property Assessment: * Condition evaluation, Updates and features that add value, Issues that might affect pricing or buyer response, Recommended improvements (if any)

Pricing Strategy: * Realistic price range based on condition and comps, Discussion of what the market will actually bear, Strategy for attracting serious buyers quickly

This is where reality meets expectations, and it's the most important part of the process.

Let's Talk About Pricing (The Honest Version)

Here's where many sellers get surprised, frustrated, or defensive, so let's address it head on.

Your online estimate is probably wrong.

Zillow's "Zestimate," Redfin's algorithm, Realtor.com's valuation, these are automated guesses based on broad data.

They don't see inside your home. They don't know about: Your deferred maintenance, Your outdated kitchen or bathroom, Your foundation crack or roof issues, Your beautiful renovation or recent updates, The specific condition of your property vs the comps

It might feel good to believe your house is worth $250,000 because that's what the algorithm says. But if comparable homes in better condition recently sold for $230,000, and yours needs $20,000 in work, the market won't care what Zillow thinks.

Here's what actually matters: recent comparable sales of similar properties in similar condition.

A professional agent will show you: What similar homes have actually sold for (not just what they were listed for) * How your property's condition compares to those sales, What updates or issues affect value in your market, What price range will attract serious buyers right now

This is apples to apples comparison.

If you're comparing your 3 bedroom, 2 bath home built in 1975 with original kitchen and bathrooms to a 3 bedroom, 2 bath home built in 1975 that was fully renovated two years ago, those are not the same apple. One is worth significantly more than the other.

Your agent's job is to show you where your property actually sits in the market, not where you want it to sit, but where buyers will realistically value it.

Why Pricing Strategy Matters More Than You Think

Here's what happens when properties are priced incorrectly:

Scenario 1: Overpriced Listing

You list at $250,000 because that's what you need to make your next move work, even though comps suggest $230,000 is more realistic.

- Week 1: Lots of clicks, some showings. Buyers tour it and move on.
- Week 2 3: Showing activity drops. Serious buyers have already seen it and passed.
- Week 4: The listing is now "stale." Days on market are accumulating.
- Week 5 6: You drop the price to $240,000. But now buyers wonder, "What's wrong with it?", Week 7 8: Another price drop to $235,000. More days accumulate. Buyer confidence erodes.
- Week 9 10: You finally price it at $230,000 where it should have started, but now it's been sitting for two months and the perception is damaged.

You might eventually sell it for $225,000 because you've lost negotiating leverage and momentum.

Scenario 2: Properly Priced Listing

You list at $230,000 from day one based on realistic comps and honest condition assessment.

- Week 1: Strong showing activity. Multiple buyers inter-ested.
- Week 2: You receive 2 3 offers. Buyers recognize the value

and don't want to lose it.
- Week 3: You're under contract, possibly at $235,000 because competition pushed the price up.
- Week 4 6: Inspection, appraisal, closing process moves smoothly.

You sell faster, for more money, with less stress.

Pricing appropriately is not pessimism, it's strategy. An overpriced listing sits on the market, accumulates days, and loses credibility. A correctly priced listing generates immediate interest, creates competition, and often results in offers at or above asking price.

The goal isn't to list at the highest number you can imagine. The goal is to list at the price that generates activity, attracts serious buyers, and closes the deal in a reasonable timeframe.

When Is a Property Better Suited for Investors?

Here's something most sellers don't realize until they're in the middle of it: even when you list on the open market, you might still sell to an investor.

And that's okay. Sometimes an investor is the best buyer for your property.

If your home: Needs a new roof, Has significant foundation or structural issues, Requires major electrical or plumbing work, Has a dated kitchen/bathroom that needs full renovation, Has code violations or deferred maintenance

...then retail buyers (people looking for a home to live in) may not be interested, or they'll make offers at investor level pricing anyway after their inspection reveals the issues.

The question becomes: Do you want to list it publicly, go

through the process, and potentially end up with an investor offer anyway? Or do you want to sell it off market to a proven investor network from the start?

There's no wrong answer. It depends on your timeline, your tolerance for the listing process, and whether you believe there's a retail buyer out there who will see the value despite the condition.

A good agent will be honest with you about this. If your property is likely to attract investors no matter which path you take, it's worth understanding that upfront so you can make an informed decision about which process makes sense.

Step 2: Property Preparation

If you decide to list, the next step is preparing the property for market.

This might include: Cleaning and decluttering, Essential. Buyers need to see the space, not your stuff. * Minor repairs, Fixing things that are broken or cosmetically distracting, Addressing safety issues, Peeling paint, handrails, trip hazards (especially important for FHA financing) * Landscaping/curb appeal, First impressions matter, Professional photography, How your property appears online determines whether buyers schedule showings

We'll dive deeper into what's worth doing (and what's not) in Chapter 5, but the key principle is this: you're not renovating the house, you're preparing it to show well relative to its price point.

If you're selling a $150,000 starter home, you don't need granite countertops. You need it to be clean, functional, and well maintained. If you're selling a $400,000 home, expectations are higher.

Your agent should guide you on what will move the needle and what won't.

Step 3: Going Live, Marketing and Showings

Once the property is ready: Professional photos are taken, The listing goes live on the MLS, Zillow, Realtor.com, and other platforms, Showings are scheduled, Buyers and their agents tour the property, Open houses may be held if appropriate for your market, Feedback is collected, What are buyers saying? Are they interested? Any concerns?

This phase typically lasts 2 4 weeks in a normal market. If you're priced right and the property shows well, you should see activity quickly.

If you're getting lots of showings but no offers, that's feedback. Usually it means: The price is too high for the condition, Something about the property is turning buyers away (smell, clutter, obvious issues) * The competition is stronger

A good agent will troubleshoot with you and make adjustments if needed.

Step 4: Offers and Negotiation

When offers come in, your agent will help you evaluate: **Price** Is it at, above, or below asking? * **Contingencies** Is the buyer financing, or paying cash? How long is their inspection period? * **Timeline** When do they want to close? * **Earnest money** How much are they putting down as a good faith deposit? * **Buyer strength** Are they pre approved? Is their lender reputable?

You'll negotiate terms, accept the strongest offer, and go

under contract.

Step 5: Under Contract, The Real Work Begins

Being under contract doesn't mean the deal is done. This is where many sellers get surprised by how much can still happen.

The buyer will typically: 1. Conduct a home inspection, A licensed inspector evaluates every major system and component 2. Request repairs or credits, Based on the inspection report 3. Get an appraisal (if financing) The bank needs to confirm the property is worth what they're lending 4. Finalize their loan approval, The lender reviews all documentation

Any of these can create complications: The inspection reveals issues the buyer wants addressed, The appraisal comes in lower than the sale price, The buyer's financing hits a snag

Your agent will help you navigate these situations, but this is why the 30 60 day timeline exists, there are moving parts, and not all of them are under your control.

Step 6: Closing

If everything goes smoothly, you'll reach closing day. You'll sign paperwork, transfer title, and receive your proceeds.

The timeline from listing to closing is typically 30 60 days, sometimes longer depending on buyer financing and any issues that arise.

The Difference Professional Guidance Makes

Here's why working with an experienced professional matters:

They've seen your situation before. Whatever you're dealing with, foreclosure timelines, inherited property, reverse mortgage deadlines, short sale complexity, they've guided someone through it. You're not the first, and that experience matters.

They know the market. Not the Zillow algorithm version. The real version, what buyers are actually paying, what sells quickly vs what sits, how to position your property competitively.

They have systems and networks. Whether it's connecting you with reliable cash buyers or marketing your property to the widest pool of retail buyers, they have infrastructure you don't.

They handle complexity. Short sales, probate, liens, code violations, inspection negotiations, these aren't simple DIY projects. Professionals deal with them every day.

They protect your interests. A good agent or investor partner isn't trying to take advantage of you, they're trying to get you the best outcome possible given your situation and timeline.

Setting Expectations: What This Process Requires From You

Whether you're selling for cash or listing on the market, here's what you'll need to provide:

Honest information about the property's condition. Don't hide issues, they'll come up eventually, and it's better to address them upfront.

Realistic expectations about pricing and timeline. If you need $200,000 to make your next move work, but the property is realistically worth $160,000, we need to have that conversation early so you can adjust your plans accordingly.

Responsiveness. Whether it's signing paperwork, providing access for showings, or answering questions, timely communication keeps the process moving.

Trust in the process. If you hire a professional, let them do their job. They're not perfect, but they have experience you don't.

What Comes Next

By now you understand what working with a professional team looks like, whether you're exploring a cash sale or listing your property for maximum value.

The next chapters will dive deeper into the practical details: How to prepare your property (and what's actually worth doing) * What home inspections look for (and why pre sale inspections are your secret weapon) * The listing process in detail, What to expect when you're under contract

But before we get into those specifics, let's talk about one of the most common mistakes sellers make, the FSBO trap. Because understanding why "doing it yourself" often costs more than hiring a professional will save you time, money, and frustration.

Let's dive into that next.

6

Preparing the Property to Sell

If you've decided to list your property on the market, the next question is inevitable: What do I need to do to get it ready?

This is where sellers often make costly mistakes, either by doing too much and spending money they won't recover, or by doing too little and leaving money on the table.

The goal of this chapter is simple: help you understand what's actually worth doing, what's a waste, and how to think strategically about preparing your property based on its price point and condition.

We call this "lipstick on a pig", not because your property is a pig, but because the strategy is about making smart, targeted improvements that enhance appeal without over investing in a property you're about to sell.

Let's break it down.

The Core Principle: Don't Remodel a House You're Not Living In

Here's the first rule: You are not renovating this property for yourself. You're preparing it for sale.

That distinction matters.

When you renovate a home you're living in, you're making choices based on your taste, your lifestyle, and your long term enjoyment. You might splurge on a luxury feature because you'll enjoy it for years.

When you're preparing a property to sell, you're making choices based on one question: Will this improvement generate more in sale price than it costs?

Most major renovations don't. Kitchen remodels, bathroom gut jobs, new flooring throughout, these are expensive projects that rarely return dollar for dollar value in a sale. You might spend $25,000 on a kitchen renovation and only see the sale price increase by $10,000 to $15,000. That's not a good investment when you're selling.

The goal is strategic enhancement, not transformation.

You're trying to: Make the property show well, Remove obstacles that turn buyers away, Address issues that kill deals or trigger renegotiations, Present the property as clean, functional, and well maintained

You're not trying to make it the nicest house on the block. You're trying to make it competitive at its price point.

The Five Impact Categories: Where to Focus Your Effort

When preparing a property for sale, focus on these five areas. They deliver the highest return for the least investment.

1. Cleaning and Decluttering

This is the highest impact, lowest cost improvement you can make.

Deep clean everything: * Floors, walls, windows, baseboards, Bathrooms and kitchens (these get scrutinized) * Carpets (professional cleaning or replacement if they're beyond saving) * Appliances (inside and out) * Light fixtures and ceiling fans

Declutter ruthlessly: * Remove excess furniture. Rooms should feel spacious, not crowded. * Clear countertops. Buyers want to see space, not your stuff. * Minimize personal items. Family photos, collections, quirky decor, pack it up. Buyers need to envision their life in the space, not yours. * Organize closets and storage. Buyers will open them. Overflowing closets signal "not enough storage."

Think of it this way: you're staging the property, not living in it. Every item that remains should serve a purpose, either making the space feel larger, brighter, or more functional.

Cost: $200 $500 for professional cleaning, or your own time

Impact: Massive. A clean, decluttered home shows significantly better in photos and in person.

2. Fresh Paint

Paint is one of the best investments you can make when selling.

Why it matters: * Fresh paint makes everything look newer and cleaner, It covers scuffs, marks, and stains, It neutralizes bold or dated colors, It's relatively inexpensive for the impact it delivers

What to paint: * Any room with scuffed, dirty, or boldly colored walls, Trim and doors that are dinged up or yellowed, Exterior (if it's peeling or faded, more on this below)

Color strategy: * Stick with neutral colors: soft whites, light grays, warm beiges, Avoid bold accent walls, trendy colors, or anything polarizing, Neutral doesn't mean boring, it means broadly appealing

The FHA Peeling Paint Rule:

This is critical, especially if your property is in a lower price range where buyers often use FHA financing.

FHA loans require properties to meet health and safety standards. Peeling paint is considered a safety hazard (potential lead paint exposure in homes built before 1978), and FHA appraisers will flag it.

If your property has peeling paint, exterior or interior, and the buyer is using FHA financing, the deal can be delayed or killed entirely until the issue is fixed. The appraiser won't approve the loan until the peeling paint is scraped, primed, and repainted.

Don't let a $200 paint job kill a $150,000 sale.

Even if you think your buyers won't use FHA financing, it's worth addressing peeling paint because: It looks neglected, It signals deferred maintenance, It can scare away buyers who worry about what else has been ignored

Cost: $500 $2,000 depending on how much needs painting

Impact: High. Fresh paint transforms a space and eliminates an FHA red flag.

3. Minor Repairs and Functional Fixes

Fix the small stuff that buyers will notice and use against you in negotiations.

Address these: * Leaky faucets or running toilets, Broken cabinet handles or drawer pulls, Cracked light switch covers or missing outlet covers, Loose handrails or wobbly banisters, Doors that don't close properly, Windows that don't open or are cracked, Broken screens or missing storm windows, Burned out light bulbs (sounds obvious, but check every fixture)

Buyers notice these details. More importantly, home inspectors notice them and list them in reports. When buyers see a long list of "deferred maintenance" items, they start thinking: What else has been neglected?

Fixing these issues upfront shows that the property has been cared for.

Cost: $300 $800 for most minor repairs

Impact: Medium to high. Prevents buyer concerns and inspection renegotiations.

4. Curb Appeal and Landscaping

First impressions are formed in the first 10 seconds. If the exterior looks neglected, buyers assume the interior is too, even if it's not.

Focus on: * Mowing, edging, and trimming, Overgrown grass and weeds signal neglect, Pruning shrubs and trees,

Clean up overgrowth, remove dead branches, Adding mulch to beds, Fresh mulch makes landscaping look cared for, Cleaning walkways and driveways, Pressure wash if stained or dirty, Front door and porch, Paint or clean the front door, add a new welcome mat, clean light fixtures, House numbers and mailbox, Replace if faded or broken

You don't need to install a professional landscape design. You just need the property to look maintained and welcoming.

Cost: $200 $600 for basic landscaping cleanup

Impact: High. Buyers form opinions before they even walk inside.

5. Light Fixtures and Hardware Updates

Small cosmetic updates can modernize the look of a property without major expense.

Consider: * Replacing dated or broken light fixtures (especially in kitchens and bathrooms) * Updating cabinet hardware (pulls and knobs) Modern hardware can make old cabinets look better, Replacing old faucets if they're corroded or ugly, Updating doorknobs if they're tarnished or broken

These are inexpensive upgrades that improve the overall feel of the property. Buyers notice when fixtures look old and cheap. They also notice when details look updated and intentional.

Cost: $200 $500 for selective updates

Impact: Medium. Adds polish without major investment.

What NOT to Spend Money On

Just as important as knowing what to fix is knowing what to skip. Here are common wastes of money when preparing to sell:

New flooring throughout Unless the existing flooring is destroyed (not just dated), don't replace it. Clean or repair what's there. If carpet is beyond saving, replace only the worst areas.

Kitchen or bathroom remodels Full renovations are expensive and rarely return full value. Unless something is actively broken or non functional, leave it. Buyers will have their own taste anyway.

High end finishes or luxury upgrades Granite countertops, custom tile, designer fixtures, these don't make sense if you're selling. You won't recover the cost.

Landscaping overhauls Professional landscape design, new sod, elaborate plantings, these are unnecessary. Basic maintenance and cleanup are sufficient.

New appliances (unless broken) If your appliances work, leave them. If one is broken, consider whether replacing it makes sense for your price point. For a $150,000 house, don't buy a $1,200 stainless steel refrigerator. Buy a basic functional one for $500 or sell without it.

Structural or major system work (usually) Foundation repairs, new roofs, HVAC replacement, these are expensive and complicated. In most cases, it's better to price the property to reflect the needed work rather than invest tens of thousands upfront. There are exceptions, but they're rare.

The guiding principle: Don't spend money on improvements that won't move the needle on buyer interest or sale price.

Tailoring Your Strategy to Your Price Point

What makes sense for a $150,000 starter home is different from what makes sense for a $400,000 move up home.

For lower priced properties ($100k $200k):

Buyers at this price point expect functional and clean, but not luxury. Focus on: Deep cleaning, Fresh neutral paint, Addressing any FHA safety issues (peeling paint, handrails, trip hazards) * Basic landscaping, Minor repairs

Do NOT invest in high end upgrades. Your buyers aren't expecting granite and stainless steel. They're expecting affordable and functional.

For mid range properties ($200k $350k):

Buyers here expect a bit more polish. The same fundamentals apply, but the standards are higher: Everything should be clean and well maintained, Consider updating dated light fixtures or hardware, Address cosmetic issues that make the property feel tired, Make sure the property competes with other homes in this range

For higher priced properties ($350k+):

Expectations increase. Buyers here are comparing your property to others in the same range, and they expect: High quality presentation, Modern finishes (even if not brand new) * Attention to detail, Professional staging or design consultation may be worth considering

Even at this level, you're not doing full renovations. You're making strategic improvements that position the property competitively.

When to Do Almost Nothing: Selling As Is

Here's a scenario where minimal preparation makes sense:

If your property needs significant work (major systems failing, structural issues, extensive deferred maintenance), and you: Don't have the funds to address it, Don't have the time or capacity, Are targeting investor buyers anyway

...then doing cosmetic improvements might not make sense. You're not going to paint over a failing foundation or landscaping around a roof that needs replacement.

In this case, the strategy is different: price it for its condition and market it to investors who buy as is properties.

You're not competing with retail buyers at this point, you're competing with other distressed properties. Cleanliness still matters (it helps with showings), but major prep work won't change the buyer pool.

Be honest about this with your agent. If the property genuinely needs $40,000+ in work, spending $3,000 on paint and landscaping might not deliver a return. It might make more sense to price it lower and sell it faster to an investor who was going to renovate anyway.

The Pre Sale Inspection Strategy (A Preview)

We're going to cover this in detail in the next chapter, but it's worth mentioning here:

Consider getting a pre sale home inspection.

A pre sale inspection costs $300 $500, and it tells you exactly what a buyer's inspector will find. Armed with that information, you can: Decide which issues are worth fixing before listing, Price the property to account for known issues, Avoid surprises during the buyer's inspection that lead to renegotiations

This is one of the smartest strategies for sellers, especially if you're unsure about the property's condition. We'll break down why it's your secret weapon in Chapter 6.

A Simple Preparation Checklist

Here's a quick reference guide for what to do before listing:

Essential (Do These): * Deep clean the entire property, Declutter and remove excess furniture/personal items, Paint any rooms with scuffed, dirty, or bold colored walls, Fix peeling paint (interior and exterior) * Address minor repairs (leaks, broken fixtures, etc.) * Mow, edge, and clean up landscaping, Clean or replace carpets if heavily stained, Replace burned out light bulbs, Ensure all doors and windows function properly, Clean gutters and downspouts, Remove trash, debris, and stored items from yard

Consider (If Budget Allows): * Update dated light fixtures in key areas, Replace old cabinet hardware, Pressure wash exterior, driveway, walkways, Add fresh mulch to landscaping beds, Paint or replace front door if it's in bad shape, Get a pre sale inspection

Skip (Usually Not Worth It): * Full kitchen or bathroom renovations, New flooring throughout, Luxury upgrades or high end finishes, Landscaping overhauls, New appliances (unless broken)

The Bottom Line: Smart Investment, Not Overspending

Preparing your property to sell is about strategy, not perfection.

You're not trying to create your dream home. You're trying to present a clean, functional, well maintained property that appeals to buyers at your price point and removes obstacles that could kill the deal.

Every dollar you spend should have a clear purpose: either increasing buyer interest, improving showing quality, or preventing inspection issues that lead to renegotiations.

If you're unsure what's worth doing, this is where your agent's experience matters. They've seen what works, what doesn't, and what generates return in your specific market and price range.

Now that you understand how to prepare your property, let's talk about one of the smartest moves you can make before listing: the pre sale inspection. It's a secret weapon that can save you thousands and prevent deals from falling apart.

Let's dive into that next.

7

Pre Sale Inspections (Your Secret Weapon)

Here's a scenario that plays out constantly in real estate:

You list your property. It shows well. You get an offer. You're excited. You go under contract.

Then the buyer's home inspection happens.

Three days later, you receive a five page inspection report listing dozens of issues, some legitimate, some minor, some purely informational. The buyer's agent emails: "Based on the inspection findings, my clients are requesting $8,000 in repairs or credits."

Now you're in a negotiation you didn't see coming. You thought the hard part was getting the offer. Turns out, the inspection is where deals get renegotiated, or fall apart entirely.

Most sellers are blindsided by this. They shouldn't be.

This chapter explains what home inspections actually involve, how buyers use them as leverage, and why getting your own pre sale inspection is one of the smartest strategic moves you can make.

What Home Inspectors Actually Look For

A home inspection is a comprehensive evaluation of the property's major systems and components. A licensed inspector spends 2 4 hours examining the property from top to bottom, inside and out.

Here's what they're evaluating:

Exterior

Roof: Condition, age, missing or damaged shingles, flashing, gutters, downspouts

Foundation: Cracks, settlement, water intrusion signs

Siding and trim: Damage, rot, peeling paint, proper caulking

Grading and drainage: Proper slope away from foundation, standing water issues

Driveways and walkways: Cracks, trip hazards, deterioration

Decks and porches: Structural integrity, railings, stairs

Structural

Framing: Visible damage, sagging, improper modifications

Basement/crawl space: Moisture, mold, structural issues, pest evidence

Attic: Proper ventilation, insulation, roof decking condition, evidence of leaks

Systems

Electrical: Panel condition, wiring, grounding, GFCI outlets where required, proper amperage

Plumbing: Water pressure, visible leaks, pipe condition, water heater age and condition, drain function

HVAC: Heating and cooling systems, age, operation, maintenance evidence, ductwork condition

Water heater: Age, operation, proper venting, signs of leaks

Interior

Windows and doors: Operation, seals, condition, safety features

Walls, ceilings, floors: Cracks, stains, damage, levelness

Kitchens and bathrooms: Fixture operation, evidence of leaks, ventilation

Stairs and railings: Safety, proper height, secure attachment

Smoke and CO detectors: Presence and function

Additional Items

Appliances: (if included) Basic operation test

Fireplace/chimney: Visible condition, proper venting

Garage: Door operation, safety sensors, structural condition

The inspector documents everything. They take photos. They make notes. They test every system they can access.

And at the end, they produce a detailed report.

How Inspection Reports Are Structured (The Three Categories)

Inspection reports typically categorize findings into three levels:

1. Good Condition / No Issues

These are the systems and components working as intended with no concerns. This is what you want to see.

Example: "The HVAC system is operating properly and appears well maintained. Estimated age: 5 years."

2. Needs Attention / Monitor / Repair Recommended

These are issues that aren't urgent but should be addressed, or items showing wear that will need attention soon.

Examples: "Minor cracks in driveway. Monitor and seal as needed.", "Water heater is 12 years old, nearing end of typical lifespan (10 15 years). Plan for replacement.", "Gutters have debris buildup. Clean to ensure proper drainage."

3. Safety Concern / Immediate Repair / Non Functional

These are serious issues, safety hazards, non functioning systems, or conditions requiring immediate attention.

Examples: "GFCI outlets not present in bathroom. Electrical safety concern.", "Handrail on basement stairs is loose and improperly secured. Fall hazard.", "Furnace is not operating. Professional HVAC evaluation required.", "Evidence of active water intrusion in basement."

Buyers and their agents focus on categories 2 and 3.

Even if your property has 50 items listed as "good condition," buyers will zero in on the 15 items flagged as needing attention or repair. That list becomes their negotiation leverage.

How Buyers Use Inspections to Renegotiate

Let's be clear about what's happening during a home inspection: It's not just an information gathering exercise. It's a negotiation reset.

Here's the typical sequence:

Day 1 7: You and the buyer negotiate and agree on a price. You're both happy. Contract signed.

Day 8 14: The buyer's inspection happens. The inspector finds issues (they always do).

Day 15 17: The buyer receives the inspection report and discusses it with their agent.

Day 18: You receive an email: "Based on inspection findings, the buyer is requesting the following repairs OR a $7,500 credit at closing."

Now you're back in negotiation. The buyer is using the inspection findings to either: Request that you fix specific items before closing, Request a credit (money back) to cover the cost of repairs they'll do themselves, Renegotiate the sale price downward, Walk away from the deal entirely (if the inspection contingency allows it)

This is completely normal and legal. The inspection contingency exists specifically to give buyers this opportunity. It protects them from buying a property with unknown issues.

But from the seller's perspective, it's frustrating, especially when you're surprised by the findings or when buyers use minor issues to push for major credits.

The Buyer's Leverage

Here's what gives buyers negotiating power at this stage:

Time and effort invested. By this point, you've had the property off the market for 1 2 weeks. You've turned away other potential buyers. You've mentally moved on. The idea of starting over is unappealing.

The inspection report as evidence. It's not just the buyer complaining, it's a licensed professional documenting issues. That carries weight.

The threat of walking away. If you don't negotiate, the buyer can use their inspection contingency to cancel the contract and get their earnest money back. You're back to square one.

Emotional momentum. Buyers get cold feet. Inspections give them a reason to second guess the purchase. Even minor issues can feel major when buyers start thinking "What else is wrong that the inspector didn't find?"

Common Inspection Negotiation Scenarios

Scenario 1: The Reasonable Request
The inspection finds a legitimate issue, a failing water heater, a roof leak, a non functioning furnace. The buyer asks you to fix it or provide a credit.

This is reasonable. These are real issues that affect the property's value and function. Most sellers negotiate in good faith here.

Scenario 2: The Nitpick List
The inspection lists 30 minor items: caulking gaps, a loose

doorknob, a slow drain, weatherstripping that needs replacing. The buyer's agent sends a list requesting you address "all inspection items."

This is unrealistic. Not every inspection finding is a legitimate repair demand. Some items are routine maintenance. Some are informational. Good agents help sellers push back on unreasonable requests.

Scenario 3: The Aggressive Renegotiation

The buyer uses the inspection as an excuse to renegotiate the entire deal. They claim the inspection revealed more issues than expected and request a $10,000 price reduction, even though the issues are minor or cosmetic.

This is frustrating but happens. Sometimes buyers have remorse. Sometimes they're testing leverage. Sometimes their agent is inexperienced and overreacting.

Scenario 4: The Deal Killer

The inspection reveals a major issue, foundation problems, mold, significant structural damage, that neither party anticipated. The repair cost is substantial. The buyer walks away.

This is the worst case scenario, but it happens. The property goes back on the market, and you're required to disclose the issue to future buyers. Your negotiating position is now weaker.

The Pre Sale Inspection Advantage: Flipping the Script

Here's the game changing strategy: Get your own inspection before you list the property.

A pre sale inspection costs $300 $500 (depending on property size and location). For that investment, you get:

A complete picture of your property's condition You know exactly what an inspector will find before any buyer sees it.

Time to address issues strategically Instead of scrambling to respond to a buyer's demands under time pressure, you can decide calmly which issues are worth fixing and which to disclose and price accordingly.

Elimination of surprises There's no "gotcha" moment during the buyer's inspection because you already know what's there.

Stronger negotiating position When buyers raise inspection concerns, you can say, "We're aware of that. Here's what we've addressed, and here's why we priced the property to account for the rest."

Fewer failed deals When major issues are discovered during a buyer's inspection, deals fall apart. When you know about issues upfront, you can disclose them and attract buyers who are comfortable with them from the start.

Higher buyer confidence Some sellers even provide their pre sale inspection report to buyers (with a disclaimer). It shows transparency and can reduce buyer anxiety.

How It Works in Practice

Let's say you're preparing to list your home. You hire an inspector for $400. They produce a report with these findings:

Major Issues: * Water heater is 14 years old and showing signs of corrosion (replacement recommended) * GFCI outlets missing in bathrooms (electrical code issue) * Basement has minor moisture intrusion during heavy rain

Minor Issues: * Several windows have broken seals (fogging between panes) * Gutters need cleaning, Caulking around tub needs replacement, Handrail on deck stairs is loose

Now you have choices:

Option 1: Fix Everything

You spend $1,800: Replace water heater: $1,200, Install GFCI outlets: $300, Tighten handrail and re caulk: $100, Clean gutters: $200

You list the property with confidence that the major issues are resolved. When the buyer's inspection happens, the report is clean. No renegotiation.

Option 2: Fix Strategically

You spend $1,500 fixing the critical items (water heater, GFCI outlets) but disclose the basement moisture issue and price the property $3,000 lower to account for it.

Buyers who tour the property know about the basement issue upfront. The ones who make offers are comfortable with it. When their inspection confirms the moisture issue, it's not a surprise, it's already priced in.

Option 3: Disclose and Price Accordingly

You decide not to fix anything, but you disclose all known issues and price the property $5,000 $7,000 lower.

You attract investors or handy buyers who are comfortable

tackling the repairs themselves. They're getting a deal on price in exchange for taking on the work.

All three options are valid. The key is that YOU'RE making the strategic decision, not reacting under pressure to a buyer's demands after you're already under contract.

Creating Your Punch List: What to Fix, What to Disclose

Once you have a pre sale inspection report, work with your agent to create a strategic punch list.

Priority 1: Safety and Code Issues

Fix these. They're red flags that scare buyers and can cause financing problems (especially FHA loans).

- Missing GFCI outlets, Handrails that are loose or missing, Electrical hazards, Non functioning smoke/CO detectors, Peeling paint (FHA issue)

Cost: Usually $200 $800
   Benefit: Eliminates deal killers

Priority 2: Functioning Systems

If a major system isn't working, you have to address it, either by fixing it or pricing accordingly.

- Non functioning HVAC, Water heater at end of life or leaking, Roof leaks, Plumbing leaks

Cost: Varies widely ($500 $5,000+)
Benefit: Prevents buyers from walking away or demanding huge credits

Priority 3: Cosmetic and Maintenance Items

These are judgment calls. Fix the ones that are cheap and improve showing quality. Disclose the rest.

- Caulking gaps, Minor plumbing drips, Loose fixtures, Gutter cleaning

Cost: Minimal ($100 $300)
Benefit: Shows the property is well maintained

What to Disclose Instead of Fix

Some issues aren't worth fixing before you sell: Older systems that still function (8 year old furnace, 10 year old roof) Disclose the age, price accordingly, Cosmetic wear, Worn carpet, dated fixtures, Buyers can see this themselves, Non urgent items, Minor cracks, small roof shingle issues, Disclose and let buyers decide

The strategy is: Fix what creates fear or kills deals. Disclose what's visible or minor. Price everything into your listing strategy.

The Real Cost Benefit Analysis

Let's look at real numbers:

Without Pre Sale Inspection:

You list at $230,000. You get an offer for $228,000. You're excited.

Buyer's inspection finds: Water heater issue, Missing GFCI outlets, Basement moisture

Buyer requests $6,000 in credits.

You negotiate down to $4,500. You also spend $300 on electrician emergency visit to install GFCI outlets so the deal doesn't fall apart.

Net result: You lose $4,800 and spend a week stressing about whether the deal will survive.

With Pre Sale Inspection:

You pay $400 for pre sale inspection. It finds the same issues.

You spend $1,500 fixing the water heater and GFCI outlets before listing.

You disclose the basement moisture issue and price the property at $227,000 to account for it.

You get an offer for $227,500. Buyer's inspection confirms what's already disclosed. No renegotiation.

Net result: You spend $1,900 upfront but avoid the $4,500 credit. You net $2,600 more and have zero stress during the inspection period.

The pre sale inspection saves you money and protects your deal.

When Pre Sale Inspections Make the Most Sense

Pre sale inspections aren't necessary for every property, but they're highly valuable when:

You're unsure about the property's condition. If you inherited the property, haven't lived there in years, or know there are some issues but don't know the full extent, a pre sale inspection gives clarity.

The property is older or has deferred maintenance. Homes built before 1990, properties with older systems, or homes where maintenance was delayed, these benefit from knowing what's lurking before buyers find it.

You want to avoid surprises and renegotiations. If your timeline is tight or you can't afford to have deals fall apart, the inspection eliminates uncertainty.

You're in a competitive market. In a seller's market, offering a pre inspected home can differentiate your listing and attract serious buyers who value transparency.

You're selling to retail buyers (not investors). Retail buyers are more likely to be scared off by inspection findings. Investors expect issues. If your property is targeting families or first time buyers, pre sale inspections reduce their anxiety.

When to Skip It

Pre sale inspections are less valuable when:

The property is brand new or nearly new. If major systems are under warranty and everything is modern, there's less to worry about.

You're selling to investors as is. Investors expect to find issues. They're factoring repairs into their offer already. A pre sale inspection won't change their approach.

You already know about major issues and you're pricing accordingly. If you're fully aware the roof needs replacement and you've priced the property $8,000 below market to reflect it, a pre sale inspection just confirms what you already know.

How to Use Pre Sale Inspections Strategically

If you decide to get a pre sale inspection, here's how to maximize its value:

Hire a reputable inspector. Ask your agent for recommendations. You want someone thorough, not someone who'll go easy on the property.

Attend the inspection. Walk through with the inspector. Ask questions. Understand what they're seeing and why it matters.

Review the report with your agent. Go through the findings together and create a strategic plan: what to fix, what to disclose, how to price.

Keep receipts for repairs you make. If you fix issues, document it. Show buyers and their agents that you've addressed concerns proactively.

Decide whether to share the report with buyers. Some sellers provide the report upfront (with a disclaimer that buyers should still do their own inspection). Others use it internally to guide their strategy. Discuss with your agent what makes sense for your market.

Be prepared to disclose known issues. Once you have the inspection report, you're legally obligated to disclose material defects. Don't try to hide problems, it can create liability.

The Bottom Line: Knowledge Is Power

Most sellers approach home inspections reactively, they wait for the buyer's inspection and then scramble to respond.

Smart sellers approach inspections proactively, they get ahead of the issues, address what matters, and position their property strategically.

A $400 pre sale inspection can save you thousands in credits, prevent deals from falling apart, and give you confidence throughout the selling process.

It's one of the best investments you can make when preparing to sell.

Now that you understand how to prepare your property and protect yourself from inspection surprises, let's walk through what happens when you actually list the property: how marketing works, what to expect during showings, and how the offer process unfolds.

That's what we'll cover next.

8

Listing Your Property the Right Way

You've prepared the property. You've addressed the issues that matter. You understand your pricing strategy. You're ready to list.

Now the real work begins.

Listing a property isn't just about putting a sign in the yard and waiting for buyers to show up. It's about strategic marketing, managing access and showings, interpreting feedback, and positioning your property to stand out in a competitive marketplace.

This chapter walks you through what happens from the day your listing goes live to the day you receive an offer. You'll understand what to expect, what's normal, what's concerning, and how to navigate the process successfully.

Let's start at the beginning.

Before the Listing Goes Live: Professional Photography

Here's a reality most sellers don't think about: The majority of buyers will decide whether to see your property based on photos alone.

They're scrolling through Zillow or Realtor.com on their phone. They see your listing thumbnail. They either click to see more, or they keep scrolling.

You have about 2 seconds to capture their attention.

This is why professional photography matters. Not because you need magazine quality images, but because you need photos that make buyers want to see more.

What Makes Good Listing Photos

Bright and well lit. Dark, shadowy photos make properties look uninviting. Professional photographers use proper lighting and editing to make spaces look open and welcoming.

Wide angle but not distorted. You want to show the space accurately. Too wide and rooms look fake. Too narrow and they look cramped.

Clean and staged. This goes back to Chapter 5, decluttered, organized spaces photograph better. Buyers focus on the property, not your belongings.

Highlight the best features. Kitchen, bathrooms, living areas, outdoor spaces, any recent updates, these should be prominently featured.

Honest representation. Don't try to hide flaws with clever angles. Buyers will see them in person, and you'll lose credibility.

The Photo Sequence Strategy

The first photo is the most important, it's often the exterior or the most attractive room. This is what buyers see in search results.

After that, the sequence should flow logically: Exterior/curb appeal, Entry/living room, Kitchen, Dining area, Bedrooms, Bathrooms, Special features (finished basement, deck, etc.) * Yard/outdoor space

Most listings include 25 40 photos. Too few and buyers wonder what you're hiding. Too many and they lose interest.

DIY Photos vs Professional: The Reality

Some sellers try to save money by taking their own photos with a smartphone. Here's the honest truth: It usually hurts more than it helps.

Unless you have photography experience and proper equipment, your photos won't compete with professionally shot listings. Buyers compare properties side by side. If your listing looks amateurish next to similar properties with professional photos, you'll get fewer showings.

Professional photography costs $150 $300 in most markets. For that investment, you dramatically improve your listing's first impression. It's worth it.

Marketing Exposure: Where Buyers Actually Find Your Property

Once photos are ready, your listing goes live. But where, exactly, does it go?

The MLS: The Foundation

The Multiple Listing Service (MLS) is the database that real estate agents use to share listings. When your agent enters your property into the MLS, it becomes visible to: Every agent in your market (and their buyer clients) * National real estate websites through syndication

The MLS is the single most important marketing tool. It's not public facing, but it feeds all the public platforms buyers actually use.

Syndication: Where Buyers Search

Once your listing is in the MLS, it automatically syndicates (publishes) to major real estate websites: Zillow, Realtor.com, Redfin, Trulia, Homes.com, And dozens of smaller sites

This is where 90%+ of buyers find properties. They're not driving around looking for yard signs. They're searching online, filtering by price, location, and features, and clicking on listings that appeal to them.

Your listing appears across all these platforms simultaneously, usually within 15 minutes to a few hours of being entered into the MLS.

Additional Marketing

Depending on your agent and market, additional marketing might include: Social media promotion, Facebook, Instagram posts targeting local buyers, Email campaigns, Sent to agents and potential buyers in their database, Yard sign and directional signs, Still effective for drive by visibility, Flyers and brochures, Available at showings and open houses, Agent networking, Your agent reaching out directly to agents with active buyers

But make no mistake: the MLS and syndicated websites do the heavy lifting. Everything else is supplemental.

Showings and Access: Making It Easy for Buyers to See Your Property

Once your listing is live, buyers will want to see it. Your job (and your agent's) is to make that as easy as possible.

The Lockbox System

Most listings use an electronic lockbox attached to the front door. This allows buyer's agents to access the property for showings without you being present.

How it works: * The lockbox contains your house key, Buyer's agents use a special access code or electronic device to open the lockbox, They show the property to their clients, The lockbox tracks who accessed it and when (your agent gets a notification)

Why this matters: The easier it is for agents to show your property, the more showings you'll get. If buyers have to schedule appointments days in advance or coordinate with your schedule, you'll lose opportunities.

Occupied vs Vacant Properties

If you're still living in the property:
You'll need to be flexible about showings. Buyers want to see properties when it's convenient for them, evenings, weekends, sometimes last minute.

Tips for occupied properties: Keep the property show ready at all times (or as much as possible) * Be prepared to leave during showings (buyers are more comfortable exploring without you there) * Secure valuables and personal items, Keep pets contained or take them with you

If the property is vacant:
Showings are easier to coordinate, but you'll need to: Keep utilities on (heat, electric, water) so the property is functional for showings, Maintain the property (mow lawn, check for issues, keep it clean) * Consider security measures (vacant homes can be targets for theft or vandalism)

Showing Notifications and Feedback

Your agent should notify you when showings are scheduled and follow up afterward to get feedback from the buyer's agent.

Typical showing notification: "Showing scheduled for tomorrow at 3pm. Agent: Sarah Johnson with ABC Realty. Buyer feedback will be available within 24 48 hours."

Typical feedback responses: * "Clients loved the kitchen and layout. Pricing seems fair. They're considering an offer.", "Property shows well but needs updating. Clients are still looking.", "Too small for their needs, but appreciated the tour.", "Pricing seems high for the condition."

This feedback is valuable. If you're getting lots of showings but no offers, the feedback tells you why, and whether you need to adjust price or address specific concerns.

Open Houses vs Private Showings

There are two main ways buyers view properties: private showings (scheduled individually) and open houses (where the property is open to the public during set hours).

Private Showings

This is the most common approach. Buyer's agents schedule one on one appointments to show the property to their clients.

Advantages: * Serious, pre qualified buyers, Personalized attention from their agent, Flexible scheduling, Better security (you know who's entering your property)

Disadvantages: * Requires more coordination, Multiple disruptions if you're living there

Open Houses

An open house is typically held on a weekend for 2 3 hours. The property is open to anyone who walks in, no appointment needed.

Advantages: * Attracts neighbors and curious buyers who might not schedule a private showing, Creates urgency (if multiple people tour at once, it signals interest) * Less disruptive than multiple individual showings

Disadvantages: * Less control over who enters (some people are just curious, not serious buyers) * Security concerns (you'll want to secure valuables) * Not always effective in slower markets

When open houses make sense: * New listings (first weekend on market) * High traffic neighborhoods where foot traffic is likely, Unique or high interest properties, Seller's markets where competition is strong

When to skip them: * Properties in remote locations with low traffic, Markets where private showings are the norm, Security concerns outweigh potential benefits

Your agent will recommend the strategy that makes sense for your market and property.

The First Two Weeks: The Critical Window

The first two weeks after your listing goes live are the most important.

This is when your property gets maximum visibility. Buyers who have been actively searching get notified of your new listing. Agents check new listings daily to show their clients. Your property appears at the top of search results (sorted by "newest").

This is when serious buyers act. If your property is priced right and shows well, interested buyers will schedule showings quickly, often within the first few days.

This is when you'll know if your pricing strategy is working.

What Strong Activity Looks Like, Multiple showing requests within the first 48 72 hours, Positive feedback from buyer's agents, Questions about offer process and timeline, Multiple showings scheduled in the first week, An offer (or multiple offers) within 7 14 days

If this is happening, your pricing and presentation are working. Stay the course.

What Weak Activity Looks Like, Few or no showing requests in the first week, Feedback mentioning price concerns, Lots of online views but no showing requests, Showings that don't convert to offers

If this is happening, something needs to adjust, usually price, but sometimes presentation or marketing messaging.

The Danger of "Days on Market"

Every day your property sits on the market without selling, the "days on market" (DOM) counter ticks up. This number is visible to buyers and their agents.

Fresh listings (0 14 days) signal opportunity. Buyers think: "New listing! Let's check it out before someone else does."

Listings with 30 45+ days on market signal a problem. Buyers think: "Why hasn't this sold yet? What's wrong with it?"

The longer a property sits, the more negotiating power shifts to buyers. They assume you're motivated (or desperate) and will lowball offers.

This is why pricing right from day one matters so much. You get maximum leverage in those first two weeks. If you overprice and then reduce, you've already lost momentum.

Reading the Market: What Feedback Actually Means

After showings, you'll receive feedback from buyer's agents. Learning to interpret this feedback is critical.

"Property shows well, but pricing seems high."

Translation: Buyers like the property but think they can get similar homes for less, or they're waiting for a price reduction.

Action: Review comps again. If similar properties are priced lower or selling for less, you may need to adjust. If you're priced correctly, wait, sometimes buyers test this feedback to see if you'll drop the price.

"Great house, but not quite what they're looking for."

Translation: This is a polite brush off. It doesn't mean anything is wrong, the buyers just have different needs or preferences.

Action: None. This is normal. Not every buyer is right for every property.

"Needs too much updating for their budget."

Translation: The property is dated or needs work, and buyers in this price range expect move in ready.

Action: Either update the property (probably not worth it at this stage) or adjust the price to reflect the condition.

"Interested but want to see a few more properties first."

Translation: They're still shopping. You're on their shortlist but not their top choice yet.

   Action: Stay patient. Sometimes these buyers come back with an offer after comparing other properties.

"Clients loved it. They're discussing an offer."

Translation: This is the feedback you want. An offer is likely coming soon.

   Action: Be ready to respond. Offers can come within hours or days of this feedback.

The Offer Process: How Offers Come In

When a buyer wants to make an offer, their agent prepares a written purchase agreement and submits it to your agent.

What's Included in an Offer

A typical offer includes:

   Purchase price What the buyer is offering to pay

   Earnest money deposit A good faith deposit (usually 1 3% of purchase price) showing the buyer is serious

   Financing contingency Details about how the buyer is paying (cash, conventional loan, FHA, VA, etc.) and how long they have to secure financing

   Inspection contingency The timeframe for conducting a home inspection and requesting repairs or credits

   Appraisal contingency If financing, the property must appraise at or above the sale price

Closing date When the transaction will finalize

Additional terms Seller concessions, included appliances, repairs, etc.

Evaluating Offers: It's Not Just About Price

When an offer comes in, you and your agent evaluate:

Price Is it at, below, or above asking? How does it compare to your bottom line?

Buyer strength Are they pre approved for financing? Is their lender reputable? How much earnest money are they putting down?

Contingencies Are they asking for a long inspection period? Are they making the offer contingent on selling their current home?

Timeline Does their closing date work for your needs?

Flexibility Are they asking for seller concessions, repairs, or other accommodations?

A strong offer isn't always the highest price. Sometimes a slightly lower offer from a cash buyer with no contingencies is better than a higher offer from a buyer with shaky financing and a long inspection period.

Your agent will help you evaluate the strength of each offer and negotiate terms that protect your interests.

Multiple Offers: The Seller's Advantage

If your property is priced well and shows competitively, you might receive multiple offers, sometimes simultaneously.

This is the best case scenario. Competing buyers often

increase their offers to stand out. You can: Request "highest and best" offers (asking all buyers to submit their strongest offer by a deadline) * Negotiate with your preferred buyer, Accept the offer that's best overall (not necessarily the highest price)

Multiple offers give you leverage and can push the final sale price above asking.

Timeline: Day 1 30 of the Listing Process

Here's what a typical timeline looks like:

Day 0: Pre Launch * Final photos, listing description finalized, Pricing strategy confirmed, Lockbox installed, sign ordered

Day 1 3: Launch * Listing goes live on MLS and syndicates to all major sites, First showing requests typically come in within 24 48 hours, Agent outreach to network begins

Day 4 10: Peak Activity * Multiple showings scheduled, Feedback starts coming in, Serious buyers often make offers in this window

Day 11 20: Evaluation Phase * If no offers yet, review activity and feedback, Adjust strategy if needed (price, presentation, marketing) * Continue showings and follow up

Day 21 30: Decision Point * If still no offers, more aggressive adjustments may be needed, If offer is accepted, you move into the "under contract" phase

The goal is to have an accepted offer within the first 14 21 days. Properties that sell quickly almost always perform better than properties that linger on the market.

What If Nothing Is Happening?

If you've been on the market for 2 3 weeks with minimal activity, it's time to diagnose the problem:

Low online views? * Photos may be poor quality, Listing description may not be appealing, Property may not be showing up in searches (check price filters, are you just above a common threshold like $200k?)

High online views but no showings? * Price is likely too high for what's visible in photos, Property condition apparent in photos is deterring buyers

Showings but no offers? * Price is too high for the in person experience, Property has issues that become apparent during showings, Feedback should tell you what's wrong

Offers but too low? * Market is telling you the property is overpriced, Buyers are calculating repair costs and adjusting their offers accordingly

Your agent should be proactive about diagnosing and addressing these issues. Don't let a listing sit without action.

The Bottom Line: Listing Is Active, Not Passive

Listing your property successfully requires attention, responsiveness, and strategic thinking.

- Keep the property show ready, Be flexible with showings, Monitor feedback closely, Stay in regular communication with your agent, Be willing to adjust if the market is telling you something

When done right, the listing process leads to offers, and

that's when the next phase begins: going under contract and navigating the path to closing.

That's what we'll cover next.

9

Under Contract, What Happens Next

You've received an offer. You've negotiated terms. You've signed the purchase agreement.

Congratulations, you're under contract!

But here's what many sellers don't realize: being under contract doesn't mean the deal is done. It means you've entered the most complex phase of the transaction, where multiple things need to happen correctly for the sale to actually close.

This chapter walks you through what happens between "offer accepted" and "keys handed over." You'll understand the timeline, the potential roadblocks, and how to navigate this phase successfully.

Let's break down what comes next.

Understanding "Under Contract"

When you accept an offer and both parties sign the purchase agreement, the property goes "under contract" or "pending."

This means: The property is no longer actively on the market, You've agreed to sell to this specific buyer, The buyer has a defined period to complete due diligence (inspection, appraisal, financing) * Both parties are legally bound to the contract terms (with specific contingencies that allow either party to cancel under certain conditions)

The typical timeline from contract to closing is 30 45 days, though it can be shorter (cash deals) or longer (complex financing, needed repairs).

The Five Phases of Being Under Contract

Let's walk through what happens, step by step.

Phase 1: Home Inspection (Days 1 14)

The buyer will schedule a home inspection, usually within the first 7 14 days after going under contract. This is their opportunity to have a licensed inspector evaluate the property's condition.

What Happens During the Inspection

The inspector examines every major system and component (as we discussed in Chapter 6). They produce a detailed report categorizing issues as: Good condition, Needs attention/monit oring, Safety concern/immediate repair needed

The buyer receives this report and has decisions to make.

Five Possible Buyer Responses

Response 1: No Inspection Requests

The buyer reviews the report, accepts the property's condition, and moves forward with no repair requests.

This is rare but happens when: The property is in excellent condition, The buyer is experienced and expected the issues found, The buyer is motivated and doesn't want to risk losing the property

Response 2: Reasonable, Specific Repair Requests

The buyer asks you to address legitimate issues that affect the property's function or safety.

Example: "Please repair the leaking water heater and install missing GFCI outlets in bathrooms."

This is the most common scenario. The buyer isn't asking for cosmetic updates, they're asking for functional problems to be fixed.

Response 3: Request for Credit in Lieu of Repairs

The buyer asks for a credit at closing instead of you making repairs.

Example: "In lieu of repairs, we're requesting a $2,500 credit at closing."

Buyers often prefer this because: They can control the quality of repairs, They can shop for contractors, It's cleaner than coordinating repairs during the transaction

Response 4: Aggressive Renegotiation

The buyer uses the inspection report to request major price reductions or extensive repair lists, sometimes beyond what's reasonable based on the findings.

Example: "Based on the inspection, we're requesting $8,000 in credits or we'll need to reconsider our offer."

This is frustrating, especially if the issues are minor or were already reflected in the pricing. Good agents help sellers push back on unreasonable demands.

Response 5: Cancellation

The buyer discovers something in the inspection that makes them uncomfortable, and they use their inspection contingency to cancel the contract and get their earnest money back.

This happens when: Major issues are discovered (foundation problems, mold, structural damage) * The buyer gets cold feet and uses the inspection as an excuse, The repair costs are substantial and the buyer can't or won't proceed

This is the worst outcome, the property goes back on the market, you've lost 1 2 weeks, and you now have to disclose the inspection findings to future buyers.

Your Response Strategy

When the buyer submits inspection requests, you have options:

Accept the requests If they're reasonable and you want to keep the deal moving.

Negotiate Counter with what you're willing to do. "I'll fix the water heater but not the cosmetic items."

Offer a credit If you don't want to coordinate repairs. "I'll provide a $1,500 credit instead of making repairs."

Push back If the requests are unreasonable. "The issues you're raising are minor maintenance items that don't warrant credits."

Hold firm If you believe the buyer is overreaching. "The property is priced for its condition. I'm not providing additional concessions."

Your agent will help you evaluate what's fair and strategically sound.

Phase 2: Appraisal (Days 7 21)

If the buyer is financing the purchase (not paying cash), their lender will order an appraisal. This typically happens within the first 1 2 weeks after going under contract.

What Is an Appraisal?

An appraisal is an independent evaluation of the property's market value, conducted by a licensed appraiser hired by the buyer's lender.

The lender needs to confirm that the property is worth at least the amount they're lending. If the buyer is purchasing for $200,000 with a 10% down payment, the lender is lending $180,000. They want to make sure the property is actually worth $200,000 (or more) so their loan is secure.

Three Possible Appraisal Outcomes

Outcome 1: Appraisal Meets or Exceeds Sale Price

The appraiser determines the property is worth $200,000 (or more). The deal proceeds as planned. This is the ideal outcome.

Outcome 2: Appraisal Comes in Low

The appraiser determines the property is worth $195,000, but the contract price is $200,000.

Now there's a $5,000 gap. Someone needs to make up that difference.

Options to resolve: * Seller lowers price to $195,000 (you take the hit) * Buyer brings an extra $5,000 cash to closing (they cover the gap) * You meet in the middle (seller lowers to $197,500, buyer brings extra $2,500) * Buyer's agent challenges the appraisal (provides additional comps to support higher value) * Deal falls apart (buyer cancels using appraisal contingency)

Outcome 3: Appraisal Comes in Significantly Low

The appraiser determines the property is worth $180,000, but the contract price is $200,000.

A $20,000 gap is substantial. The deal is at serious risk. The buyer likely can't (or won't) bring that much extra cash, and you probably aren't willing to drop the price that much.

The deal often dies in this scenario.

Why Low Appraisals Happen

You overpriced the property. If the market doesn't support your price, the appraiser's comps will reflect that.

Market shift. If the market has softened since you priced the property, appraisals can come in lower than recent comps suggested.

Appraiser is conservative. Some appraisers use stricter criteria or older comps, resulting in lower valuations.

The property is unique. If there aren't good comparable sales, appraisers struggle to support higher values.

Phase 3: Buyer Financing (Days 1 30)

While the inspection and appraisal are happening, the buyer is working on securing their loan. This process takes 3 5 weeks on average.

What the Lender Is Doing

Verifying income and employment Pay stubs, tax returns, employment verification

Reviewing credit Credit score, debt to income ratio, payment history

Verifying assets Bank statements showing down payment and closing cost funds

Ordering appraisal As discussed above

Processing the loan Submitting everything to underwriting for approval

What Can Go Wrong

Even if the buyer is "pre approved," things can derail their financing:

Job loss or income change If the buyer loses their job or their income drops, the loan won't be approved.

New debt If the buyer opens new credit cards, finances a car, or takes on other debt during the transaction, their debt to income ratio can be affected.

Credit issues Late payments, collections, or credit score drops can kill the loan.

Insufficient funds If the buyer doesn't have enough money for down payment and closing costs (and it's discovered late), the deal can't close.

Documentation problems Missing paperwork, unexplained deposits, or self employment income issues can delay or kill financing.

Red Flags to Watch For

The buyer's lender requests extensions If closing keeps getting pushed back, it's often a financing issue.

Communication goes quiet If you stop hearing updates from the buyer's agent or lender, something might be wrong.

Last minute document requests If the lender is scrambling for additional paperwork close to closing, approval isn't certain.

Your agent should stay in touch with the buyer's agent and lender to monitor progress and catch problems early.

Phase 4: Title Search and Closing Preparation (Days 1 30)

While the buyer is handling their inspection and financing, the title company (or attorney, depending on your state) is working on the title search and closing preparation.

What Is a Title Search?

A title search is a review of public records to confirm. You legally own the property, There are no liens, claims, or encumbrances that would prevent clear transfer of ownership, There are no legal disputes over the property

The title company searches: Deed records, Mortgage records, Tax records, Court records, Judgment and lien records

Common Title Issues (And How They're Resolved)

Outstanding liens Unpaid contractors, HOA dues, tax liens
   Resolution: These are typically paid from your closing proceeds. The title company calculates what's owed and deducts it from your payout.
   Mortgage payoff discrepancies Your mortgage balance doesn't match what you thought
   Resolution: The title company requests an updated payoff statement from your lender.
   Ownership disputes Questions about who actually owns the property (often happens with inherited property)
   Resolution: Legal documentation proving ownership. This can delay closing.
   Easements or restrictions Rights of way or deed restrictions that weren't disclosed
   Resolution: These are disclosed to the buyer. Depending on severity, the buyer may proceed or renegotiate.
   Most title issues are resolvable, but they can add time to the process. If your property has a complicated ownership history, inherited title, or known liens, address these early.

Phase 5: Final Walkthrough and Closing (Days 28 45)

As you approach the closing date, final preparations happen.

The Final Walkthrough (24 48 Hours Before Closing)

The buyer (and their agent) will do a final walkthrough of the property, typically the day before or morning of closing.
   What they're checking: * The property is in the same

condition as when they made the offer, Any agreed upon repairs were completed, All fixtures and appliances that were supposed to stay are still there, The property is vacant and clean (if that was the agreement)

Potential Last Minute Problems

Property isn't in agreed upon condition Damage occurred, or something is broken that wasn't before.

Repairs weren't completed If you agreed to fix something and didn't, the buyer can refuse to close.

Items are missing If appliances, fixtures, or other items were supposed to stay but are gone, the buyer can demand credits or delay closing.

Property isn't clean/vacant If you agreed to have it cleaned out and ready, and it's not, the buyer can push back.

Avoid these problems by: Completing agreed upon repairs and keeping documentation, Not removing anything that's included in the sale, Ensuring the property is ready per the contract terms

The Closing

Closing is the final step. You'll meet at the title company (or attorney's office) to sign paperwork, transfer ownership, and receive your proceeds.

What happens: * You sign the deed transferring ownership, You sign closing documents, The buyer signs their loan documents (if financing) * Funds are transferred, You receive your proceeds (usually by wire or cashier's check) * You hand over keys, garage remotes, alarm codes, and any other access items

Timeline: Closings typically take 30 60 minutes for the seller (longer for the buyer, who has more paperwork).

Once it's done, the property is no longer yours. The transaction is complete.

Common Roadblocks and How to Handle Them

Even with everything going smoothly, roadblocks can occur. Here's how to navigate them:

Roadblock 1: Inspection Disputes

Problem: Buyer requests excessive repairs or credits

Solution: Negotiate. Separate legitimate issues from nit-picking. Offer reasonable compromises. Know when to hold firm.

Roadblock 2: Low Appraisal

Problem: Appraisal comes in below contract price

Solution: Evaluate whether lowering the price makes sense, or if the buyer should cover the gap. Consider challenging the appraisal if comps support a higher value.

Roadblock 3: Buyer's Financing Falls Through

Problem: Buyer's loan is denied or delayed

Solution: Set a deadline for the buyer to secure financing or you'll put the property back on the market. Don't wait indefinitely.

Roadblock 4: Buyer Gets Cold Feet

Problem: Buyer hesitates or looks for reasons to cancel

   Solution: Stay firm. If they're using contingencies appropriately, you may have to let them walk. If they're trying to cancel without valid reason, enforce the contract.

Roadblock 5: Title Issues Delay Closing

Problem: Title problems take longer to resolve than expected

   Solution: Work with the title company to resolve quickly. Communicate clearly with the buyer about the delay.

Your Responsibilities While Under Contract

As the seller, you have specific obligations during this phase:

Stay Accessible

Respond to requests from your agent, the buyer's agent, inspectors, appraisers, and the title company promptly.

Maintain the Property

Don't let the property deteriorate. Continue maintenance, pay utilities, and keep it in the condition it was in when the buyer made the offer.

Complete Agreed Upon Repairs

If you committed to fixing something, get it done on time. Don't delay or skip agreed upon repairs.

Cooperate with Access

Allow the buyer, inspectors, appraisers, and contractors access as needed. Schedule around their needs.

Prepare for Move Out

Start packing, arrange your move, and prepare to vacate by the closing date.

Communicate with Your Agent

Stay in regular contact. Let them know about any concerns or changes in your situation.

The Typical Timeline: Week by Week

Here's what a standard 30 45 day contract period looks like:

Week 1: Contract to Inspection, Contract signed, earnest money deposited, Home inspection scheduled and completed, Inspection report received by buyer, Buyer submits any repair requests or credits

Week 2: Inspection Resolution, Negotiate inspection requests, Agree on repairs, credits, or price adjustments, Inspection contingency is satisfied (or buyer cancels)

Week 3: Appraisal and Loan Processing, Appraisal conducted, Appraisal report received by lender, Resolve any appraisal issues, Buyer's loan moves through underwriting

Week 4: Underwriting and Title, Loan receives final underwriting approval, Title search completed, any issues resolved, Closing date confirmed

Weeks 5 6 (if needed): Final Steps, Final walkthrough scheduled, Closing documents prepared, Utilities arranged for transfer, Final walkthrough completed, Closing day

If the Deal Falls Apart

Despite best efforts, some deals don't make it to closing. If your deal falls through:

The Property Goes Back on Market

You'll need to relist. Communicate quickly with your agent about strategy.

Days on Market Increases

The time you were under contract counts as days on market in most MLS systems. This can hurt perception.

You Must Disclose Known Issues

If the buyer's inspection revealed problems, you now have to disclose those to future buyers.

Future Buyers Will Wonder Why

Be prepared to explain honestly why the first deal fell through. "Buyer's financing fell through" or "Inspection revealed issues buyer wasn't comfortable with" are common, understandable explanations.

Adjust Your Strategy

If the deal died due to price or condition issues, consider adjusting before relisting.

The Bottom Line: Stay Engaged and Patient

Being under contract is the most uncertain phase of the transaction. Things can still go wrong. But if you: Stay responsive and communicative, Maintain the property, Negotiate fairly on inspection requests, Complete what you committed to, Work with your agent to address problems

...the vast majority of contracts close successfully.

The finish line is in sight. Stay focused, and you'll get there.

In the next chapter, we'll address one of the biggest mistakes sellers make, trying to sell the property themselves (FSBO) to "save the commission." We'll show you why that strategy usually costs more than it saves.

Let's dive into that next.

10

FSBO: The Myth of Saving Money

"If I sell it myself, I'll save the commission."

This thought crosses the mind of almost every seller at some point. It's understandable. When you're looking at a potential 5 6% commission on a $200,000 property, that's $10,000 to $12,000, it feels like a lot of money to "give away."

The logic seems simple: list the property yourself, handle the showings, negotiate with buyers, and keep that commission in your pocket. It's called FSBO, "For Sale By Owner", and thousands of sellers attempt it every year.

Some succeed. Most don't. And many of those who "succeed" actually lose more money than they saved.

This chapter isn't about convincing you that you can't sell your own property. You absolutely can. People do it. But it's about helping you understand what you're actually taking on, what you're giving up, and why the commission you're trying to save often costs you far more than hiring a professional would have.

Let's look at the reality behind FSBO.

Why FSBO Is Tempting (And Why It Makes Sense to Consider)

Before we get into the problems with FSBO, let's acknowledge why it's appealing in the first place.

The commission feels like "dead money." You're selling your property. You're doing the work of preparing it. Why should you pay someone thousands of dollars to facilitate something you could theoretically do yourself?

You know your property better than anyone. You've lived there. You know its strengths. You know the neighborhood. Why wouldn't you be the best person to sell it?

You've seen enough HGTV. Selling a house doesn't look that complicated. Take some photos, post it online, show it to interested buyers, negotiate a price, sign some paperwork. How hard could it be?

The commission is substantial. On a $250,000 home, a 6% commission is $15,000. That's a new car. That's months of mortgage payments. That's a meaningful chunk of money.

These are all reasonable thoughts. The desire to keep that commission makes sense.

The question is: What does that commission actually cover? And what happens when you don't have it?

The Math That Seems to Make Sense

Here's the simple math that draws people to FSBO:

Sale price: $225,000 Traditional commission (6%): $13,500 FSBO commission (none): $0 Savings: $13,500

On paper, it looks obvious. Sell it yourself, save $13,500.

But this math assumes two things: 1. You'll sell the property for the same price an agent would have 2. The only value an agent provides is worth exactly the commission amount

Both of these assumptions are almost always wrong.

What FSBO Sellers Actually Give Up

1. Maximum Market Exposure

The MLS (Multiple Listing Service) is the database where nearly all properties are listed and where agents search for homes for their buyer clients.

FSBO sellers don't have direct access to the MLS. You can pay for limited MLS exposure through certain services, but you won't have the same reach as a traditional listing. More importantly: Your property won't syndicate automatically to Zillow, Realtor.com, Redfin, and other major platforms the way MLS listings do, Buyer's agents won't see your property when searching for their clients, Your property won't appear in automated alerts that go to active buyers in your price range

The buyer pool is dramatically smaller. You're limited to people who happen to drive by your yard sign, see your Craigslist post, or stumble across your listing on a FSBO website.

Real estate agents represent 85 90% of buyers. When you're FSBO, you're essentially invisible to those buyers unless their agent specifically seeks out your listing, and most won't bother because working with FSBO sellers is more complicated.

2. Professional Marketing

Real estate marketing isn't just "post it online and wait."

Professional agents provide: High quality photography (which we covered in Chapter 7, this matters enormously) * Strategic listing descriptions that highlight features and appeal to the right buyers, Pricing analysis based on comprehensive market data, Staging advice and presentation strategy, Coordination of showings and open houses

FSBO sellers typically: Use smartphone photos (which look amateurish compared to professional listings) * Write descriptions that don't highlight what buyers actually care about, Price based on what they need or what Zillow says, not what the market data supports, Struggle to coordinate showings because they're doing it manually without a system

Your listing competes with dozens (or hundreds) of other listings. If yours looks amateurish or is poorly marketed, it gets ignored, even if the property itself is great.

3. Negotiation Expertise

Negotiating a real estate transaction isn't like negotiating the price of a used car. It's a multi layered process involving: Initial offer and counteroffer, Inspection findings and repair requests, Appraisal issues, Financing contingencies, Contract terms and timelines, Legal compliance and disclosures

Professional agents negotiate dozens of transactions per year. They know when to hold firm, when to compromise, and how to structure terms that protect your interests.

FSBO sellers negotiate once (maybe a few times if they've sold properties before). They're emotionally invested in the property and the outcome. They don't know what's standard, what's reasonable, or what's a red flag.

This inexperience costs money, either in accepting terms that don't serve you or in scaring away buyers by being too rigid or unrealistic.

4. Buyer Representation and Cooperation

Here's something many FSBO sellers don't realize: Most buyers work with agents.

When a buyer has an agent and they want to see your FSBO property, you now have to deal with that agent. And here's the catch: that agent expects to be compensated for representing their buyer.

So your options are: 1. Offer to pay the buyer's agent (typically 2.5 3%) which means you're not saving the full commission anyway 2. Refuse to pay the buyer's agent, which means most agents won't show your property to their clients

If you choose option 2, you've just eliminated 85 90% of potential buyers.

If you choose option 1, you're paying half the commission anyway, and you're still doing all the work yourself.

5. Legal Protection and Compliance

Real estate transactions involve: Contracts with specific legal language, Disclosure requirements that vary by state, Fair housing laws, Title issues and liens, Deadlines and contingencies

Agents are trained in these areas (and carry errors and omissions insurance if something goes wrong).

FSBO sellers are on their own. If you miss a required disclosure, violate fair housing laws, or mess up the contract, you're personally liable. Lawsuits can cost tens of thousands, or more.

6. Time and Stress

Selling a property takes time: Researching comparable sales and pricing, Taking photos and creating listings, Responding to inquiries (many of which are tire kickers or scammers) * Scheduling and conducting showings, Negotiating offers, Coordinating inspections, appraisals, and closing

Agents do this full time. It's their job.

For FSBO sellers, it's a second job, one they're not experienced at, don't have systems for, and are doing while managing their actual job, family, and moving logistics.

The stress and time investment are real costs, even if they don't show up in dollars.

The Hidden Costs of FSBO

Beyond what you give up, there are actual costs that FSBO sellers often don't anticipate:

1. Lower sale price

Study after study shows that FSBO properties sell for less than agent represented properties, typically 10 20% less, even after accounting for commission savings.

Why? Because FSBO sellers: Price incorrectly (often too high, which leads to sitting on the market and eventual price drops) * Have weaker negotiating position, Attract fewer buyers (less competition = less leverage) * Don't know how to create urgency or handle multiple offers

2. Longer time on market

FSBO properties take longer to sell on average, often 2 3x longer than agent listed properties.

Every extra month on the market costs you: Mortgage payments, Property taxes, Insurance, Utilities, Maintenance, Opportunity cost (what else you could be doing with that equity)

3. Marketing costs

Professional photography: $150 $300 FSBO website listing fees: $300 $500 Yard signs and marketing materials: $100 $200 Legal review of contracts: $500 $1,000+

These add up quickly, and you're still not getting professional level marketing.

4. Buyer agent compensation

As mentioned, if you want buyers with agents to see your property (which is most buyers), you'll need to offer buyer agent compensation, typically 2.5 3% of the sale price.

On a $225,000 property, that's $5,600 $6,750. You're saving maybe 2 3% by going FSBO, not 5 6%.

5. Legal risk

One missed disclosure, one fair housing violation, one contract error, and you could face a lawsuit that costs more than the commission you tried to save.

The Data: What FSBO Properties Actually Sell For

According to the National Association of Realtors, the median FSBO home sells for significantly less than agent assisted sales:

Recent NAR data shows: FSBO median sale price: around $310,000, Agent assisted median sale price: around $405,000

Now, this isn't a perfect comparison (FSBO sellers tend to have lower priced properties), but even when adjusted for property type and condition, FSBO properties consistently sell for 5 10% less than comparable agent listed properties.

Here's the math on a $200,000 property:

FSBO approach: * Expected sale price: $185,000 (assuming 7.5% less due to weaker marketing/negotiation) * Commission saved: $0 (but paying buyer agent 2.5% = $4,625) * Net proceeds after $4,625 buyer agent commission: around $180,375

Agent assisted approach: * Expected sale price: $200,000 (full market value) * Commission paid (6%): $12,000, Net proceeds: $188,000

Result: You net $7,625 MORE by using an agent, even after paying full commission.

This isn't hypothetical. This is the pattern that plays out repeatedly in the data.

The Haircut Analogy

Here's a way to think about FSBO:

You can cut your own hair.

You own clippers. You can watch YouTube tutorials. If you're patient and steady handed, you can probably give yourself a decent buzzcut.

But if you want style, precision, layers, a professional result that makes you look sharp, you go to a barber or stylist.

The barber doesn't charge $30 because you can't hold scissors. They charge $30 because: They have training and experience, They know techniques you don't, They have professional tools, They can see angles you can't, They can fix mistakes before they become disasters, They deliver results you can't replicate yourself

Selling a house works the same way.

You can absolutely list it yourself, field calls, schedule showings, and negotiate with buyers. And if everything goes perfectly and you have a simple transaction with motivated buyers who know what they're doing, you might pull it off successfully.

But if you want: Maximum market exposure, Professional presentation, Strategic pricing that generates competition, Expert negotiation that protects your interests, Legal compliance and risk mitigation, Systems that handle the complexity efficiently

...you hire a professional.

The commission isn't payment for something you can't do. It's payment for expertise, systems, and results you can't replicate on your own.

When FSBO Might Actually Make Sense

To be fair, there are situations where FSBO can work:

1. You're selling to someone you already know

If you're selling to a family member, friend, or tenant who's ready to buy, and you've agreed on price, FSBO might make sense. You're not marketing the property or finding a buyer, you're just facilitating a transaction between two parties who've already agreed.

Even here, though, many people hire an agent or real estate attorney to handle the paperwork correctly.

2. You're an experienced real estate professional yourself

If you're an agent, investor, or attorney with real estate transaction experience, you already have the knowledge and tools. FSBO makes more sense for you.

3. You're selling a unique property with a niche buyer pool

If you're selling a commercial property, vacant land, or specialty property where traditional MLS marketing isn't the primary buyer source, FSBO might work, though even in these cases, professionals often deliver better results.

4. The property is priced very low and will sell instantly

If you're pricing the property significantly below market because you need a fast sale and buyers will compete for it regardless of marketing, FSBO might not cost you much.

But for the vast majority of residential sellers trying to maximize value on a typical home, FSBO is a costly gamble.

The Professional Value Breakdown: What You're Actually Paying For

When you hire a real estate professional, here's what the commission covers:

Pre Listing Services, Comparative market analysis and pricing strategy, Property preparation consultation, Marketing plan development, Professional photography coordination, Staging advice

Marketing and Exposure, MLS listing with full syndication, Coordination across Zillow, Realtor.com, and other major platforms, Social media marketing, Email campaigns to agent networks, Signage and print materials, Open house coordination

Buyer Management, Fielding inquiries and pre qualifying buyers, Scheduling and conducting showings, Collecting and managing feedback, Managing buyer agent cooperation

Negotiation and Transaction Management, Offer review and negotiation, Contract preparation and review, Inspection negotiation, Appraisal issue resolution, Financing coordination and problem solving, Timeline management and deadline tracking

Legal and Compliance, Disclosure management, Fair housing compliance, Contract legal compliance, Title issue coordination, Risk mitigation

Closing Coordination, Working with title company and lenders, Managing final walkthrough, Resolving last minute issues, Ensuring successful closing

This isn't a passive process. Professional agents typically invest 20 40 hours per transaction, use professional tools and systems, carry insurance, and bring years of experience navigating problems you won't see coming.

The commission pays for all of this, and the results they deliver.

The Bottom Line: Commission Is Investment, Not Cost

Here's the reframe:

The commission isn't what it costs to sell your property.

The commission is what you invest to maximize your net proceeds, minimize risk, and ensure a successful transaction.

When you sell FSBO to "save" the commission, you're often trading: 5 6% in commission for 10 20% in lost sale price, Professional marketing for amateur presentation that sits on the market, Expert negotiation for emotional negotiation that leaves money on the table, Legal protection for personal liability risk, Efficient process for stressful, time consuming DIY project

Most FSBO sellers don't save money. They lose it.

And the ones who do save money often realize afterward that

the stress, time investment, and risk weren't worth the few thousand dollars they kept.

A Better Question Than "Can I Do This Myself?"

The question isn't "Can I sell this property myself?"

The question is: "What result am I trying to achieve, and what's the best way to get there?"

If your goal is: Maximum sale price, Fastest reasonable timeline, Minimum stress and risk, Professional handling of complex issues

Hiring a professional is the path.

If your goal is: Saving a few thousand dollars, Being willing to accept a lower sale price and longer timeline, Taking on significant time investment and risk, Learning as you go

FSBO might be worth trying, but go in with realistic expectations.

Final Thought: The Barber College Buzzcut vs. The Master Barber Experience

You can cut your own hair. You'll save $30.

But when you want to look your best for something that matters, a job interview, a wedding, an important event, you don't hand yourself the clippers.

You go to a professional because the result matters more than the cost.

Selling your property is one of the largest financial transactions of your life. The difference between doing it well and doing it poorly can be tens of thousands of dollars.

That's not a place to hand yourself the clippers.

In the next chapter, we'll address another source of confusion for sellers: the recent NAR lawsuit and commission changes. There's been a lot of noise and misinformation about this, so let's clear up what actually changed, and what didn't.

11

Commissions, NAR Lawsuit, and What Actually Changed

If you've been paying attention to real estate news over the past year or two, you've probably seen headlines like these:

"6% Real Estate Commission Is Dead" "Homebuyers Will Now Pay Their Own Agent Fees" "Real Estate Agents' Commissions Cut in Historic Lawsuit Settlement"

Politicians repeated these claims. News outlets ran with them. Social media amplified them.

And almost all of it was misleading or outright wrong.

Yes, there was a significant lawsuit involving the National Association of Realtors (NAR). Yes, there was a settlement. Yes, some things changed.

But no, the 6% commission didn't disappear. No, buyers aren't suddenly paying their agents out of pocket. And no, real estate professionals aren't suddenly working for drastically less.

This chapter clears up the confusion. We'll explain what the lawsuit was actually about, what changed, what stayed the same, and what it all means for you as a seller.

Let's start with the facts.

What the Lawsuit Was Actually About

The NAR lawsuit wasn't about whether commissions were "too high." It was about **how commission information was shared and whether certain practices reduced competition.**

The Core Issues

1. MLS Rules on Commission Display

Before the settlement, when a property was listed in the MLS, the listing would include the commission being offered to buyer's agents typically displayed as a percentage or dollar amount.

For example: *"Listing Agent Commission: 3% / Buyer Agent Commission: 2.5%"*

Plaintiffs argued this practice: Facilitated "steering" (agents directing clients to properties offering higher commissions) * Reduced competition by making commission rates more uniform across the market, Violated antitrust laws by effectively coordinating commission rates

2. Buyer Representation Agreements

The lawsuit also addressed whether buyers were adequately informed about agent compensation and whether they truly understood the cost of representation.

What the Settlement Required

In August 2024, NAR agreed to a settlement that changed MLS rules and industry practices:

Change #1: Commissions can no longer be advertised in the MLS.

Listing agents can no longer include buyer agent compensation as a searchable field in MLS listings. This information now must be negotiated directly between parties, not broadcast publicly in the listing.

Change #2: Buyers must sign representation agreements before touring properties.

Buyers working with agents must now sign a written agreement acknowledging the agent represents them and detailing how the agent will be compensated before the agent shows them properties.

Change #3: Increased transparency and disclosure.

Agents must more clearly disclose to buyers how they're being paid and ensure buyers understand they can negotiate agent fees.

What the Settlement Did NOT Do

It did NOT: Eliminate real estate commissions, Cap commissions at any specific percentage, Require buyers to pay their agents out of pocket, Prevent sellers from offering to pay buyer agent compensation, Change the basic economics of real estate transactions

The settlement changed disclosure and transparency requirements. It did not fundamentally restructure how agents are paid.

What Changed: The Paperwork, Not the Economics

Let's be specific about what's different now:

Before the Settlement

MLS Listings: * Seller lists property with agent, Listing agreement includes total commission (e.g., 5 6%) * Commission split is advertised in MLS (e.g., "2.5% to buyer's agent") * Buyer's agents see this when searching for properties

Buyer Representation: * Buyers often worked with agents without formal written agreements, Compensation was implied or explained verbally, Buyers assumed (often correctly) the seller would pay their agent

After the Settlement

MLS Listings: * Seller lists property with agent, Listing agreement includes compensation structure, Buyer agent compensation is NOT advertised publicly in MLS, Buyer's agents must negotiate compensation directly with listing agent or seller

Buyer Representation: * Buyers must sign a written representation agreement BEFORE touring properties, Agreement specifies how agent will be compensated, Agreement must clearly state who pays the agent (seller, buyer, or negotiated) * Buyers are explicitly informed they can negotiate agent fees

What This Actually Looks Like in Practice

Scenario 1: Seller Offers to Pay Buyer Agent

Seller lists property. In the listing agreement (which is private, not in MLS), seller agrees to compensate buyer's agent at 2.5%.

Buyer's agent contacts listing agent: "Is the seller offering buyer agent compensation?"

Listing agent: "Yes, 2.5%."

Buyer's agent shows property to their client. Transaction proceeds. Seller pays both agents at closing, just like before.

Scenario 2: Seller Does Not Offer to Pay Buyer Agent

Seller lists property with no buyer agent compensation offer.

Buyer's agent contacts listing agent: "Is the seller offering buyer agent compensation?"

Listing agent: "No, buyer's agent fee would need to be negotiated separately."

Buyer's agent discusses with their client. Options: 1. Buyer pays their agent directly 2. Buyer asks seller to include agent compensation in the offer 3. Buyer works with a different agent or no agent

In practice, Scenario 1 is still the norm. Most sellers still offer to pay buyer agent compensation because it makes economic sense (more on this below).

What Stayed the Same: Commissions Still Exist

Despite the headlines, here's what didn't change:

1. Total commission rates are similar.

Most listing agents still charge 5 6% total commission (though it varies by market and property price). This hasn't changed significantly.

2. Sellers typically still pay both agents.

It's still common and strategically smart for sellers to offer buyer agent compensation. The incentive structure that made this standard before the settlement still exists.

3. Agent compensation is still negotiable.

It always was. The lawsuit didn't create negotiability it already existed. What changed is disclosure and transparency requirements.

4. The economics of real estate transactions are unchanged.

Sellers still want maximum buyer pool. Buyers still typically lack cash to pay agents out of pocket. These fundamentals haven't shifted.

Why Sellers Typically Still Pay Buyer Agent Compensation

Here's the reality that many headlines missed: **There's a very practical reason sellers offer to pay buyer agents, and the lawsuit didn't change it.**

The Incentive Math

Most buyers don't have extra cash to pay their agent.

If a buyer is purchasing a $250,000 home, they're likely: Putting 3 10% down ($7,500 $25,000) * Paying closing costs ($5,000 $8,000) * Depleting most or all of their liquid savings

Asking them to also pay their agent $6,000 $7,500 out of pocket is often not realistic.

But seller proceeds make it easy.

When the seller pays buyer agent compensation, it comes out

of closing proceeds money the seller was getting anyway. For the buyer, it's invisible. They don't need extra cash.

The Competition Reality

If you offer buyer agent compensation, you get more buyers.

Imagine two identical properties: Property A: Seller offers 2.5% buyer agent compensation, Property B: Seller offers no buyer agent compensation

Agents will preferentially show Property A because: Their compensation is clear and guaranteed, Their buyers don't need extra cash, The transaction is simpler

Property B will get fewer showings because: Buyers would need extra cash (which most don't have) * Agents have to negotiate compensation separately (more work, more uncertainty) * Many agents will simply skip it and show easier to transact properties

Fewer showings = less competition = lower offers.

This is why most sellers still offer buyer agent compensation: It increases their buyer pool, which increases competition, which typically increases the final sale price.

The Math Works Out

Let's say you're selling for $240,000.

Option 1: Offer buyer agent compensation (2.5% = $6,000) * Attract 100% of potential buyers, Generate multiple offers due to competition, Sell for $240,000, Net after commissions (5.5% total): ~$226,800

Option 2: No buyer agent compensation * Attract maybe 30 40% of potential buyers (those with cash or willing to negotiate) * Less competition, weaker negotiating position, Sell for $230,000 (lower due to less demand) * Net after listing agent commission (3%): ~$223,100

You net $3,700 MORE by offering buyer agent compensation, even though you paid $6,000 for it, because the increased competition pushed your sale price higher.

This is why the practice continues. It's not about agents colluding or buyers being uninformed. It's about economic incentives that benefit sellers.

The "6% Is Dead" Myth

So where did the "6% is dead" headlines come from?

What Headlines Got Wrong

Claim: "The 6% commission is dead."

Reality: Commission rates were never fixed at 6%. They've always been negotiable and have always varied by market, property type, and agent. The settlement didn't change this. Some agents charge 5%, some 6%, some 7%, some negotiate custom rates. This has always been true.

Claim: "Buyers will now pay their own agents."

Reality: Buyers CAN pay their own agents, but most sellers still offer buyer agent compensation because it serves their interests. The settlement created more transparency about this, but didn't change the economic incentive.

Claim: "Agent commissions will drop dramatically."

Reality: Commission rates haven't changed significantly in most markets. Agents are still paid similarly to before. What changed is where compensation information is disclosed not the amounts.

Why the Misinformation Spread

1. Misunderstanding the settlement

Many reporters and politicians didn't fully understand what the settlement actually required vs. what it prohibited.

2. Wishful thinking

Some people wanted real estate commissions to drop and interpreted the lawsuit as achieving that goal, even though it didn't.

3. Clickbait headlines

"6% Commission Is Dead" gets more clicks than "NAR Settlement Changes MLS Disclosure Rules."

4. Conflating transparency with rate changes

The settlement increased transparency about commissions. Some people confused "talking about commissions more openly" with "commissions are lower."

What This Means for You as a Seller

Here's what you need to know practically:

You'll Still Negotiate Commissions with Your Agent

Just like before, you'll agree on: What your listing agent charges (typically 2.5 3%) * Whether you'll offer buyer agent compensation (typically 2 3%) * Total commission structure

This hasn't changed. These rates are still negotiable and vary.

You'll Likely Still Offer Buyer Agent Compensation

For the reasons explained above maximizing your buyer pool and creating competition most sellers still choose to offer compensation to buyer's agents.

Your agent will advise you on what's competitive in your market.

The Paperwork Looks Slightly Different

Commission information appears in different places in contracts than it used to. But functionally, the transaction works the same way.

Buyers Are More Informed

Buyers now sign representation agreements before touring, which means they understand their agent relationship better. This is actually good for sellers informed buyers tend to be more serious and less likely to waste time.

Transparency Is Higher

There's more explicit discussion of who's paying whom and how much. This is a positive change. Transparency reduces confusion and potential disputes.

Mythbuster Table: Headlines vs. Reality

Headline/Claim | Reality |

| |

"6% commission is dead" | Commission rates were never fixed and haven't changed significantly. Still typically 5 6% total in most markets. |

"Buyers must now pay their own agents" | Buyers CAN, but most sellers still offer buyer agent compensation because it expands buyer pool. |

"Agent commissions have been cut" | Commission amounts are similar. What changed is disclosure requirements, not rates. |

"NAR was forced to lower fees" | NAR didn't set fees. The settlement changed MLS rules, not commission amounts. |

"This lawsuit saves buyers money" | Buyers aren't seeing significant savings. Transactions work similarly to before. |

"Real estate agents are making less now" | Agents are compensated similarly. The structure shifted slightly but amounts are comparable. |

"Sellers can't pay buyer agents anymore" | Sellers absolutely CAN and typically still DO pay buyer agents. Nothing prevents this. |

"Commissions are now negotiable" | They always were. The settlement didn't create negotiability it increased transparency about it. |

The Bottom Line: More Transparency, Same Economics

The NAR settlement was about increasing transparency and eliminating practices that potentially reduced competition. **It was not about lowering commissions or fundamentally changing how real estate transactions work.**

For you as a seller, the practical impact is minimal: You'll still work with a listing agent, You'll still negotiate commission rates (as always) * You'll likely still offer buyer agent compensation (because it serves your interests) * The paperwork looks slightly different, but the process is essentially the same

The real change is transparency which is a good thing. More disclosure, clearer agreements, and better informed participants make for healthier markets.

But the economic incentives that structure real estate transactions? Those remain largely unchanged.

Moving Forward: Focus on Results, Not Headlines

If you're selling a property, don't get distracted by misleading headlines or political rhetoric about commissions.

Focus on what matters: Getting your property in front of the maximum number of qualified buyers, Pricing it correctly for your market, Negotiating effectively to protect your interests, Closing the transaction successfully and efficiently

Professional representation helps you achieve these goals. Whether the commission is structured as it was before the settlement or as it is now, the value delivered remains the same.

In the next chapter, we're going to shift from theory and process to real stories actual sellers who faced tough situations and how they navigated their options to successful outcomes.

These case studies will bring everything we've discussed into focus through real world examples.

Let's dive into those stories next.

12

Real Seller Stories

Everything we've covered so far signs it's time to sell, your options, preparing the property, inspections, the listing process can feel abstract until you see how it plays out for real people facing real decisions.

This chapter shares five actual seller stories. Different situations, different challenges, different solutions but all with one thing in common: **people who were stuck, overwhelmed, or trapped by property they owned, and who found a path forward.**

These aren't hypothetical scenarios. These are real transactions, real outcomes, and real lessons.

Let's meet them.

Case Study 1: Tiffany Wills, When a Renovation Loan Turns Into a Rescue Mission

The Setup

Tiffany had a plan. She and her boyfriend were going to build wealth together through real estate. They found a multi unit fixer property and secured a renovation loan the kind where the bank finances both the purchase and the repairs, releasing funds as work progresses.

The plan was solid: Live in one unit, Rent the others, Build equity while the property appreciated, Create cashflow and long term wealth

It was the kind of investor strategy you read about in books. And for a while, it was working.

The Problem

Then the relationship ended.

Suddenly, Tiffany was managing a multi unit renovation project alone. Her partner who had been handling much of the contractor coordination was gone. The renovation loan, which required meeting milestones to release funds, stalled. Work stopped. Bills piled up.

Worse, the property started accumulating building code violations. When work stops mid renovation, inspectors notice. What was supposed to be a wealth building asset was turning into a liability that was drowning her financially and emotionally.

The property was at serious risk of selling at a loss. The renovation loan balance was climbing (interest accruing), the property wasn't generating income, and the violations were creating legal pressure.

Tiffany was stuck. She couldn't afford to finish the renovation. She couldn't afford to keep the property. And she was terrified she'd lose everything she'd invested.

The Turning Point

Tiffany reached out for help. At that point, the property was in rough shape partially renovated, code violations stacked up, no rental income, and a clock ticking on the loan.

The first step was getting honest about the situation: What was owed on the renovation loan? * What were the outstanding violations and what would it cost to resolve them? * What was the property realistically worth in its current condition? * What were Tiffany's actual options?

The assessment wasn't pretty, but it was clear: **This property needed to be sold, and it needed to happen strategically to salvage any equity.**

The Solution

The team went to work:

Step 1: Resolve the violations. Code violations scare buyers and kill deals. A few strategic fixes cleared the most critical issues and got the property into legally marketable condition.

Step 2: Clean up and stage strategically. The property didn't need to be perfect it needed to show well enough to attract buyers who could see past the unfinished work.

Step 3: Price it realistically. This wasn't a fully renovated property competing with move in ready homes. It was priced for buyers (or investors) willing to take on a project but priced to move quickly.

Step 4: Market it properly. Professional photos, clear

messaging about the property's potential, and exposure to the right buyer pool.

The property went under contract within weeks.

The Outcome

Tiffany walked away with approximately **$10,000 in profit.**

That might not sound like a lot but consider the alternative: if the property had gone to foreclosure or sold at a distressed auction, she would have walked away with nothing. Or worse, still owed money on the loan.

Instead, she had: A clean exit from a situation that had become untenable, Cash in hand for a down payment on her next move, Her credit intact, No more sleepless nights worrying about violations, loan payments, or a property she couldn't manage

Within months, Tiffany bought a new place one that actually fit her life, her budget, and her goals. No multi unit renovation project. No partner drama. Just a home that worked for her.

The Lesson

Sometimes selling isn't about maximizing profit it's about cutting your losses, preserving what equity you can, and moving forward.

Tiffany's mistake wasn't buying the property. It was holding on too long once the situation changed. When the partnership ended and the renovation stalled, the smart move was to exit quickly. The longer she waited, the more equity eroded.

Selling became the reset button that saved her financial

future.

Case Study 2: Entry Level Condo to 1031 Exchange Level Up

The Setup

A young professional bought an entry level condo as their first home. It was small, affordable, and in a decent location. They lived there for a few years, built some equity, then moved into a larger place when their life circumstances changed.

Rather than sell the condo, they kept it as a rental. And for a while, it worked beautifully: Great tenant (long term, stable, paid on time) * Positive cashflow (rent covered mortgage, taxes, and expenses with a little left over) * Property appreciated nicely over the years

On paper, it was a textbook "buy and hold" investment.

The Problem

But equity was trapped.

The condo had appreciated significantly from the original purchase price of around $120,000 to a market value of roughly $180,000. That's $60,000+ in equity just sitting there, generating modest monthly cashflow but not working very hard.

Meanwhile, the owner was watching other investment opportunities pass by. Larger properties with better cashflow. Different markets with stronger appreciation potential. Ways to leverage that equity into something bigger.

The condo was a good investment but it wasn't the best use of capital anymore.

The Turning Point

The owner started exploring: *What if I sold the condo and reinvested the equity into something that performs better?*

The challenge was taxes. Selling an investment property triggers capital gains tax on the appreciation. At a 15 20% tax rate (federal plus state), that $60,000 gain would cost $9,000 $12,000 in taxes. That's a big chunk of equity lost to Uncle Sam.

But there's a tool designed exactly for this situation: **the 1031 exchange.**

A 1031 exchange allows you to sell an investment property and roll all proceeds into a new investment property without paying capital gains tax as long as you follow specific IRS rules and timelines.

The owner also had another advantage: **the tenant wanted to buy the condo.**

This created a perfect scenario: A ready buyer (the tenant) * No need to market the property or deal with showings, A clean transaction between parties who already had a relationship

The Solution

Here's how it worked:

Step 1: Structure the sale to the tenant. The tenant was already familiar with the property (they'd been living there for years) and was ready to buy. The sale price was fair market value $180,000.

Step 2: Execute a 1031 exchange. The owner worked with a qualified intermediary (required for 1031 exchanges) to struc-ture the sale so proceeds would roll directly into the next property without triggering capital gains.

Step 3: Identify and purchase a larger property. Within the required 1031 timeline, the owner identified and closed on a larger multi unit property in a stronger market. Purchase price: approximately $350,000 (using the proceeds from the condo sale plus additional financing).

The Outcome

The results were dramatic:

Before (Entry Level Condo): * Property value: $180,000, Monthly cashflow: ~$400 600, Annual cashflow: ~$4,800 7,200

After (Larger Multi Unit Property): * Property value: $350,000, Monthly cashflow: ~$1,200 1,400, Annual cashflow: ~$14,400 16,800

The owner roughly doubled their monthly cashflow and positioned themselves in a property with stronger long term appreciation potential.

And because of the 1031 exchange, they paid **zero capital gains tax** all equity rolled forward into the new investment.

The Lesson

Holding a rental property can be a great strategy but only if it's the right property at the right time.

Just because something is working doesn't mean it's optimal. The condo was generating cashflow, but the equity was underperforming. By selling strategically and using tools like the 1031 exchange, the owner turned a good investment into a great one.

This is what "making your next move your best move" looks

like in practice.

Case Study 3: The Inheritance That Almost Slipped Away

The Setup

An elderly homeowner passed away, leaving behind a house in a neighborhood that had seen better days. The property had been in the family for decades, but by the time of the owner's death, it was in rough shape years of deferred maintenance, outdated systems, and a lot of accumulated belongings.

Here's the problem: **The heirs didn't even know they had rights to the property.**

The deceased owner had no will. Probate was complicated. Family communication was minimal. And while the heirs were trying to figure out what they were entitled to (if anything), the property sat vacant.

Meanwhile: Property taxes went unpaid, Liens started piling up, The city flagged the property for code violations, A tax sale was scheduled

The property was on the verge of being lost entirely auctioned off to pay back taxes, with any remaining equity disappearing into a bureaucratic process the heirs didn't even know was happening.

The Problem

By the time anyone realized what was happening, the situation was urgent: The heirs had been located but weren't sure how to claim the property, Back taxes owed: several thousand dollars,

Liens from unpaid utilities and code violations, A tax sale date was on the calendar just weeks away, The property was full of the deceased owner's belongings (a full house cleanout would be required) * None of the heirs had the financial resources to pay off the liens and bring the property current

If nothing happened, the property would be sold at auction. The liens would be paid from the proceeds. Whatever equity remained (if any) would go into a lengthy legal process that the heirs may or may not ever recover.

The clock was ticking, and the heirs were about to lose thousands of dollars they didn't even know they were entitled to.

The Turning Point

A persistent real estate professional tracked down the rightful heirs and explained the situation:

"You have a property. It's worth money but it's about to be sold at a tax auction. If that happens, you lose everything. But if we act now, you can sell it, pay off the debts, and walk away with the equity."

This was news to the heirs. They thought the property was "too far gone" or that they had no claim to it. They didn't understand probate, tax sales, or their legal rights.

Information was the first step. Once they understood they had options and a ticking timeline they were ready to act.

The Solution

The strategy was straightforward but time sensitive:

Step 1: Establish legal authority. Work with a probate attorney to get the heirs legally authorized to sell the property (even without a full probate process, there are ways to expedite this in urgent situations).

Step 2: Assess the property and debts. Total up what's owed (taxes, liens, utilities) and what the property is realistically worth in as is condition.

Step 3: Sell quickly. Given the timeline and condition, listing on the open market wasn't an option. This was a cash buyer situation sell as is, close fast, pay off the debts, distribute remaining proceeds to heirs.

Step 4: Coordinate the cleanout. The property was full of belongings. The buyer agreed to handle the cleanout (reducing it from the purchase price), which removed a massive burden from the heirs.

The property sold weeks before the tax auction.

The Outcome

The heirs walked away with enough money to: Buy reliable cars, Secure stable housing, Create financial cushions they didn't have before

It wasn't life changing wealth but for people who thought they were getting nothing, it was transformational.

More importantly, they avoided: Losing the equity entirely to a tax sale, Years of legal wrangling trying to recover proceeds, The stress and confusion of not knowing what they were entitled to

The Lesson

Inherited properties come with deadlines and complications most heirs don't understand.

The difference between losing everything and walking away with equity is often just information and guidance. The heirs in this story almost lost thousands of dollars simply because they didn't know what they had or what to do about it.

If you've inherited property (or are the executor of an estate), don't wait. Don't assume "it's too complicated" or "it's too late." Get professional help early. Understand your timeline. Protect the equity.

Case Study 4: The Burned Out Landlord Who Escaped Chaos with Profit

The Setup

This story starts in 2008, during the subprime mortgage meltdown and the foreclosure crisis that followed.

A contractor had been doing work for banks rehabbing foreclosed properties so they could be resold. It was steady work during a time when many contractors were struggling. But the banks were slow to pay. Invoices piled up. The contractor was owed around $30,000 for work completed.

Then the banks made an offer: **"We can't pay you in cash right now, but we can pay you in properties."**

The contractor accepted. In exchange for the money he was owed, he received three properties on the same block in a rough neighborhood. Prices were severely depressed these properties were worth very little at the time, but they were tangible assets.

As a contractor, he figured he could fix them up over time, rent them out, and build equity as the market recovered.

And that's exactly what happened for a while.

The Problem

The properties appreciated significantly as the market recovered. What he'd acquired for essentially $30,000 in forgiven debt was now worth well over $100,000 combined. He had equity.

But the properties were in a rough area. The tenants were difficult he described them as "thuggish." They didn't pay consistently. They caused damage. They created constant stress.

Then things escalated.

One day, the contractor felt unsafe on the block during a confrontation with tenants. He had a concealed carry permit and a weapon. In the heat of the moment, he pulled it out. The police were called.

Now he was legally barred from entering one of the properties. And even the other two he couldn't safely go to the block anymore. He had "beef" with people there. It wasn't safe.

Meanwhile, the tenants figured out they had leverage. They started calling city inspectors, creating code violations to harass the owner. The properties were becoming legal liabilities.

He had equity trapped in properties he couldn't access, couldn't manage, and couldn't fix.

Stress was destroying his health. He wasn't sleeping. The properties that were supposed to build wealth were ruining his life.

The Turning Point

The contractor realized: **I need to get out of this, and I need to do it now.**

If he waited: More violations would pile up, Equity would erode through fines and legal issues, The stress would continue destroying his health, He'd eventually lose the properties entirely possibly through foreclosure or forced sale

He reached out for help. The message was clear: "I can't go to these properties. I can't deal with these tenants. I just need them gone."

The Solution

This was a perfect scenario for the cash investor network: Properties in rough condition (though with equity) * Owner couldn't access or manage them, Urgent timeline, Need for certainty and speed

All three properties were sold through the investor network within weeks. No showings. No listings. No dealing with tenants or inspectors. Just clean, fast transactions.

The contractor walked away with over $100,000 in proceeds. After paying off any remaining debts on the properties, he had significant profit far more than the $30,000 in forgiven debt he'd traded for them years earlier.

The Outcome

But here's the best part: **He didn't leave real estate. He just left the chaos.**

With the proceeds, he purchased a multi unit property in a

better area a property with stable tenants, no drama, and similar cashflow to what he'd been getting (on the rare occasions his difficult tenants actually paid).

Now he had: Equity repositioned into a better asset, Cashflow without constant stress, His health and peace of mind back, No more sleepless nights worrying about confrontations or violations

The Lesson

Equity in a property that's destroying your life isn't really equity it's a trap.

The contractor could have held on, hoping things would improve. But they wouldn't have. The tenants had taken over. The legal issues were compounding. His health was deteriorating.

Selling quickly and strategically allowed him to extract the equity, escape the chaos, and move that capital into an asset that actually served his goals.

Sometimes the best move is to liquidate a problem and turn the proceeds into a solution.

Case Study 5: The Aging Homeowner Who Chose Quality of Life Over Stairs

The Setup

She'd lived in the house for decades. It was where she raised her kids. A beautiful quad level home with character and memories.

But her kids were grown now. She was alone most of the time. And the house once perfect for a busy family was starting to feel too big, too much to maintain.

Still, it was home. She wasn't in a rush to leave.

Then one day, coming in from outside, she fell on the stairs.

The Problem

It wasn't just a fall. It was a compound fracture severe enough that it became infected. The infection led to complications. Eventually, it resulted in an amputation below the knee.

Now she had a prosthetic leg. And a quad level house full of stairs.

Every day, just getting around her own home was exhausting and dangerous. The stairs that she'd walked up and down thousands of times over the years were now obstacles. Her independence something she'd always valued was slipping away.

The house she loved had become incompatible with her life.

The Turning Point

She had resources. She wasn't desperate. But she was clear eyed about the situation: **I can't stay here.**

The decision was made. She'd sell the house and find a place that worked for her mobility something without stairs, something manageable, somewhere she could live safely and independently.

But she also had time and the ability to do it right.

The Solution

This was a textbook example of strategic preparation and execution:

Step 1: Pre sale inspection. Get the full picture of what an inspector would find. Create a punch list of items to address before listing.

Step 2: Complete targeted repairs. Address the flagged items nothing major, just the things that would come up during a buyer's inspection and create negotiation issues. A few minor fixes. Fresh paint. New carpet. Updated trim.

Step 3: Stage and clean. The house was emptied, cleaned thoroughly, and presented beautifully. It wasn't a gut remodel modern showpiece it was a well maintained, move in ready home at a competitive price point.

Step 4: Price it strategically. Based on comps and condition, price it to attract serious buyers immediately.

She stayed with her sister during the prep and staging work. It was easier than trying to live in a house being prepared for sale and it gave her time to mentally transition.

The Outcome

The house went on the market.

Within three days, it was under contract.

Inspection happened no surprises, no issues. Everything flagged in the pre sale inspection had been addressed. The buyer's inspector confirmed what was already known.

No renegotiation. No repair requests. No credits. Just a clean, smooth transaction.

The property closed 30 days after going under contract.

She walked away with over **$100,000 in equity.** And it cost less than $10,000 in prep work to get there.

With those proceeds, she purchased a condo in an elevator building. No stairs. Accessible. Safe. Everything she needed within reach.

Her quality of life improved dramatically. She regained independence. She could move around freely without fear of falling. And she was in a community with other residents her age less isolated, more connected.

The Lesson

Sometimes selling isn't about financial distress it's about life changes and adapting smartly.

This seller could have stayed in the house. She could have installed stair lifts, modified doorways, tried to make it work. But it would have been a constant struggle.

Instead, she made a clear headed decision: **sell the house that no longer serves me, and move into something that does.**

And because she did it strategically pre sale inspection, targeted repairs, proper pricing she maximized her equity and closed quickly with zero drama.

Her next move wasn't just a real estate transaction. It was a quality of life upgrade.

Common Threads: What These Stories Teach Us

These five sellers faced completely different situations: A failed renovation project, An underperforming investment property, An inherited property at risk of foreclosure, A rental nightmare destroying someone's health, A home incompatible with changing physical needs

But they all share common elements:

1. Clarity came from facing reality.

Each of these sellers reached a point where they stopped avoiding the situation and started addressing it honestly. What's really happening? What are my options? What's the best path forward?

2. Professional guidance mattered.

None of these were simple DIY transactions. Each required specific knowledge, strategic thinking, and execution that benefited from experience.

3. Timing was critical.

In several cases the inheritance, the contractor's properties waiting would have been disastrous. Acting decisively preserved equity and created better outcomes.

4. Selling wasn't failure it was strategy.

Every one of these sellers improved their situation by selling. They didn't "give up." They made smart moves that served their actual goals.

5. The next move was better than staying stuck.

Tiffany got a home that fit her life. The condo owner doubled their cashflow. The heirs got money they thought was lost. The contractor escaped chaos. The aging homeowner regained quality of life.

Selling was the bridge to something better.

Your Story Could Be Next

If you recognized yourself in any of these stories or if your situation is similar know this:

You're not stuck. You have options. And making the decision to explore those options is the first step toward a better outcome.

In the next chapters, we'll talk about what comes after the sale how to think strategically about your next move, how to protect equity, and how to make sure this transition sets you up for success going forward.

Let's keep moving.

13

Making Your Next Move the Best Move

The property is sold. You've navigated the process, closed the transaction, and received your proceeds. Congratulations.

Now comes the question: **What do you do with this opportunity?**

Because that's what liquidity is opportunity. The cash in your account isn't just money. It's options. It's flexibility. It's the ability to make choices you couldn't make when that equity was locked in a property you didn't want or couldn't manage.

This chapter isn't about telling you exactly what to do with your proceeds. Your situation, goals, and circumstances are unique. But it is about helping you think strategically about your next move so you don't waste this opportunity.

Selling the property wasn't the end goal. It was the bridge to whatever comes next.

Let's figure out what "next" looks like for you.

Taking Stock: What You're Working With

Before you make any decisions about what to do next, you need a clear picture of where you stand.

Your Financial Position

How much did you net from the sale?

After paying off the mortgage, closing costs, commissions, and any liens or repairs, what's left? This is your starting capital.

For some sellers, it's $10,000. For others, it's $100,000 or more. The amount matters, but so does how you use it.

What are your current debts?

Do you have: Credit card balances? * Student loans? * Car loans? * Other property mortgages? * Personal loans?

High interest debt (especially credit cards) eats away at your financial progress. Paying it off might be the smartest first move.

What's your monthly cashflow situation?

Are you: Comfortable with your current income and expenses? * Stretched thin and living paycheck to paycheck? * Building savings consistently?

Your cashflow determines how much flexibility you have and what kinds of moves make sense.

Your Timeline and Goals

Do you need housing immediately?

If you just sold your primary residence, you need somewhere to live. Your timeline for your next move is immediate.

If you sold an investment property, inherited property, or rental, you have more flexibility to think strategically.

What are your goals for the next 1 3 years?

Are you trying to: Build wealth? * Reduce stress and simplify? * Relocate for work or family? * Create financial stability? * Generate passive income? * Fund a business or other opportunity?

Knowing what you're working toward helps you evaluate which next move serves that goal.

Your Risk Tolerance and Capacity

How much complexity can you handle?

Some people are comfortable managing rental properties, navigating investments, or taking on renovation projects. Others want simplicity and stability.

How much risk are you willing to take?

Are you comfortable with the ups and downs of real estate markets or stock markets? Or do you need predictability and security?

There's no right answer just honest self assessment.

Common Next Moves (And What Each Accomplishes)

Here are the most common paths sellers take after closing, and what each one achieves:

1. Buy Another Primary Residence

What it is: Use your proceeds as a down payment (or full purchase) of a home you'll live in.

When it makes sense: * You just sold your current home and need housing, You want to upgrade, downsize, or relocate, You want to own rather than rent, You have stable income to support a mortgage

What it accomplishes: * Provides stable housing, Builds equity again over time, Potential tax benefits (mortgage interest deduction, capital gains exclusion on future sale) * Control over your living situation

Considerations: * You're taking on a mortgage payment (if not buying cash) * You're responsible for maintenance and repairs, You're less liquid (equity is tied up again)

2. Rent for a While

What it is: Use proceeds for other purposes and rent a place to live.

When it makes sense: * You're relocating and want to learn a new area before buying, You value flexibility and don't want to be tied to one location, You're unsure where you want to settle long term, You want to invest the proceeds elsewhere instead of in a home

What it accomplishes: * Maximum flexibility, No maintenance responsibilities, Ability to relocate easily, Frees capital for other investments

Considerations: * You're not building equity through housing, Rent payments don't provide tax benefits, You're subject to landlord decisions and rent increases, Less control over your living situation

3. Buy Investment Property

What it is: Use proceeds to purchase rental property or other real estate investments.

When it makes sense: * You want to generate passive income, You're comfortable being a landlord or hiring property management, You're looking for long term wealth building, You have the time and capacity to manage investments

What it accomplishes: * Potential monthly cashflow, Long term appreciation, Tax benefits (depreciation, deductions) * Diversification of assets

Considerations: * Requires active management (or paying a manager) * Tenant and maintenance issues arise, Capital is tied up in real estate again, Market risk and vacancy risk

4. Pay Off High Interest Debt

What it is: Use proceeds to eliminate credit cards, personal loans, or other high interest debts.

When it makes sense: * You're carrying credit card balances (15 25% interest) * You have personal loans or car loans with high rates, Your monthly debt payments are straining your budget

What it accomplishes: * Immediate "return" equal to the interest rate you're paying (20% interest debt = 20% "return" by paying it off) * Improved monthly cashflow (freed up payment amounts) * Better credit score, Reduced financial stress

Considerations: * This doesn't generate new income, Opportunity cost if you could invest at higher returns (rare to beat credit card interest rates though)

5. Build an Emergency Fund

What it is: Set aside 3 6 months of living expenses in savings.

When it makes sense: * You don't have an emergency fund, You live paycheck to paycheck, You need financial security and peace of mind, You want a cushion before making other moves

What it accomplishes: * Financial stability, Protection against job loss, medical emergencies, or unexpected expenses, Reduced stress and anxiety, Foundation for making other strategic moves

Considerations: * Money sits in low interest savings (not growing significantly) * Doesn't generate income, But provides security that's hard to quantify

6. Invest in Stocks, Bonds, or Other Assets

What it is: Invest proceeds in the stock market, bonds, mutual funds, or other financial instruments

When it makes sense: * You don't want real estate exposure anymore, You want liquidity and flexibility, You're comfortable with market volatility, You have a long term investment horizon

What it accomplishes: * Potential growth over time (historically ~7 10% annually for stocks) * Liquidity (can access funds relatively quickly if needed) * Diversification away from real estate, Passive management (no tenants, repairs, or property headaches)

Considerations: * Market volatility and risk, No physical asset or control, Taxable gains on growth (unless in retirement accounts)

7. Fund a Business or Career Change

What it is: Use proceeds to start a business, change careers, or invest in education/training.

When it makes sense: * You have a business idea you want to pursue, You need capital to launch or grow a venture, You want to change careers and need runway to retrain or transition, You're investing in skills that increase earning potential

What it accomplishes: * Potential for significant income growth, Career fulfillment and autonomy, Building a different kind of asset (business equity, skills)

Considerations: * High risk (most businesses fail) * Requires time, effort, and expertise, Capital could be lost, But potential upside is significant

Strategic Thinking: The Opportunity Cost Mindset

Here's a framework that helps clarify decisions:

Every dollar you spend or invest has an opportunity cost.

If you use $50,000 as a down payment on a house, you can't use that $50,000 to pay off debt or invest in stocks. If you pay off $30,000 in debt, you can't use it for a business venture.

The question isn't "What can I do with this money?"

The question is "What's the best use of this money given my goals, timeline, and situation?"

Example: The Debt Payoff Decision

Let's say you have: $40,000 in proceeds from the sale * $15,000 in credit card debt at 22% interest * $25,000 in student loans at 5% interest

Option 1: Pay off all debt and be debt free.

Sounds great emotionally. But financially: Paying off the student loans saves you 5% interest (low priority) * You'd have $0 left for emergency fund or other opportunities

Option 2: Pay off credit cards, keep student loans, build emergency fund.

- Pay off $15,000 in credit cards (saves 22% interest immediately)
- Keep $25,000 for emergency fund and future opportunities, Continue student loan payments (manageable at 5%)

Option 2 is almost always better. You eliminate the high interest debt that's destroying you financially, while maintaining liquidity and flexibility.

This is strategic thinking: prioritize the highest impact moves first.

Common Next Move Scenarios

Let's look at a few real world scenarios:

Scenario 1: The Fresh Start (Low Proceeds, High Debt)

Situation: * Sold distressed property, Netted $12,000 after paying off mortgage and costs, Has $8,000 in credit card debt, Currently renting, Stable job but living paycheck to paycheck

Best next move: 1. Pay off the $8,000 credit card debt immediately (eliminates 20%+ interest and frees up monthly payment) 2. Keep $4,000 as emergency fund 3. Focus on rebuilding credit and increasing income

Why this works: Eliminates the financial drain of high interest debt, creates a small safety net, and positions them to build from a stable foundation.

Scenario 2: The Upgrade (Moderate Proceeds, Stable Situation)

Situation: * Sold starter home, Netted $60,000 after payoff, Has $10,000 in savings already, Wants to buy a larger home for growing family, Good income, stable job

Best next move: 1. Use $50,000 as down payment on next home (keeps $10,000 liquid) 2. Upgrade to home that fits current needs 3. Avoid overextending on mortgage payment

Why this works: Uses proceeds for intended purpose (better housing), maintains emergency fund, improves quality of life without financial strain.

Scenario 3: The Investor Pivot (High Proceeds, Investment Goals)

Situation: * Sold problem rental property, Netted $120,000, Wants to stay in real estate but not as landlord, Has stable income from other sources

Best next move: 1. Invest $100,000 in diversified real estate investment trust (REIT) or syndication 2. Keep $20,000 liquid 3. Generate passive income without landlord responsibilities

Why this works: Stays in real estate for tax benefits and returns, but eliminates direct management headaches. Maintains liquidity for flexibility.

Scenario 4: The Simplifier (Aging, Downsizing)

Situation: * Sold large family home, Netted $180,000, Purchased smaller condo for $150,000 cash, Has $30,000 remaining, Retired, on fixed income

Best next move: 1. Keep $20,000 as emergency fund 2. Invest $10,000 in conservative income generating investments (bonds, dividend stocks) 3. Enjoy simplified, mortgage free living

Why this works: No more mortgage payment, lower maintenance, smaller space to manage, financial security cushion, supplemental income.

Worksheet: What's Your Next Move?

Use these questions to clarify your thinking:

Your Current Situation, How much did you net from the sale? __________, What debts do you have? __________, What's your monthly income/expenses? __________, Do you need housing immediately? Yes / No

Your Goals (Rank in order of importance)

- ___ Financial security / emergency fund, ___ Debt elimination, ___ Generate passive income, ___ Buy a home to live in, ___ Invest for growth, ___ Fund a business or opportunity, ___ Simplify and reduce stress, ___ Relocate to new area

Your Constraints, Do you need all proceeds liquid, or can some be tied up? __________, How much risk are you comfortable with (1 10)? _________, How much complexity can you manage (1 10)? __________, What's your timeline for your next move? _________

Your Best Next Move (Based on Above)

Write it here: _____________________________________

____

Avoiding Common Mistakes After Selling

Mistake #1: Spending Emotionally

You just closed on a sale. You have cash in your account. The temptation to splurge is real.

The trap: Buying things you don't need because "I finally have money."

The solution: Give yourself 30 days before making any major decisions. Let the emotional high of closing settle. Then make rational choices.

Mistake #2: Rushing Into the Next Property

After selling, some people feel pressure to "do something" immediately with the proceeds.

The trap: Buying the next property too quickly without proper evaluation, negotiation, or consideration of alternatives.

The solution: Unless you have an urgent timeline (need

housing), take time to explore options. Don't buy just because you have money to spend.

Mistake #3: Lifestyle Inflation

You have more cash than you've had in a while. It's tempting to upgrade everything car, living situation, spending habits.

The trap: Increasing your lifestyle costs in ways that eat up proceeds and create new financial pressure.

The solution: Improve your situation strategically, but don't inflate your baseline costs unnecessarily.

Mistake #4: Ignoring Taxes

Depending on how you use proceeds, there may be tax implications you're not considering.

The trap: Making decisions without understanding capital gains, tax deductions, or tax advantaged strategies.

The solution: Talk to a CPA or financial advisor before making major moves, especially with large proceeds.

Mistake #5: Not Having a Plan

The biggest mistake is drifting. The money sits in checking. Months pass. You're no clearer on what to do. Meanwhile, inflation erodes value and opportunities pass by.

The trap: Paralysis by analysis or avoidance.

The solution: Make a decision, even if it's just "I'm going to take 60 days to evaluate options and then commit to a direction."

The Bottom Line: Liquidity Is Power Use It Wisely

Selling that property gave you something you didn't have before: **options.**

You're no longer stuck. You're no longer trapped in a situation that doesn't serve you. You have capital, and capital creates choices.

But liquidity is only powerful if you use it strategically.

The difference between people who build wealth and people who stay stuck isn't usually how much money they have it's how they use the money they get.

Your next move can be your best move but only if you think it through, align it with your goals, and execute intentionally.

Don't waste this opportunity.

In the next chapter, we'll dive into advanced strategies for protecting and growing equity including tools like 1031 exchanges, tax optimization, and creative solutions for investors and strategic sellers.

Let's keep building.

14

Protecting Your Equity (Advanced Strategies)

Most of this book has focused on the fundamentals: understanding when to sell, preparing your property, navigating the process, and thinking about your next move.

But there are advanced strategies tools and techniques that can help you preserve more equity, reduce tax burden, and create better outcomes than a straightforward sale.

This chapter isn't for everyone. Some of these strategies are complex and require professional guidance. Some only apply to specific situations. But if you're selling investment property, dealing with significant gains, or trying to optimize your financial outcome, these tools can be worth thousands or tens of thousands of dollars.

Let's explore what's possible when you go beyond the basics.

The 1031 Exchange: Selling Without Paying Capital Gains Tax

We mentioned this briefly in Chapter 11 (the condo to larger property case study), but it's worth diving deeper because it's one of the most powerful tools available to real estate investors.

What Is a 1031 Exchange?

A 1031 exchange (named after Section 1031 of the IRS tax code) allows you to sell an investment property and reinvest the proceeds into another investment property **without paying capital gains tax on the sale.**

Normally, when you sell investment property that has appreciated, you owe capital gains tax on the profit. Depending on your income and how long you held the property, that could be 15 20% federal plus state taxes sometimes 25 30% total.

A 1031 exchange defers that tax indefinitely as long as you follow the rules.

How It Works

Here's the basic structure:

Step 1: Sell your investment property (the "relinquished property")

You list and sell your rental property, vacant land, or other investment real estate. But instead of the proceeds coming directly to you, they go to a **qualified intermediary** a neutral third party who holds the funds during the exchange.

Step 2: Identify replacement property within 45 days

You have 45 days from the sale closing to identify potential replacement properties. You can identify up to three properties of any value, or more if they meet certain IRS rules.

Step 3: Purchase replacement property within 180 days

You must close on the new property (the "replacement property") within 180 days of selling the original property. The qualified intermediary uses the proceeds from your sale to purchase the new property on your behalf, then transfers it to you.

Step 4: Meet IRS requirements

Both properties must be "like kind" (investment real estate for investment real estate residential, commercial, land, etc.). You must reinvest all proceeds and acquire property of equal or greater value to defer 100% of the tax.

If done correctly, you pay zero capital gains tax now. The tax is deferred until you eventually sell the replacement property without doing another 1031 exchange or potentially forever if you hold until death (step up in basis for heirs).

Example: The Power of Tax Deferral

Without 1031 Exchange: * Sell rental property for $300,000, Original purchase price (basis): $200,000, Capital gain: $100,000, Tax owed (assume 25% combined): $25,000, Net proceeds available for next investment: $275,000

With 1031 Exchange: * Sell rental property for $300,000, Capital gain: $100,000, Tax owed: $0 (deferred) * Net proceeds available for next investment: $300,000

You have an extra $25,000 working for you because you didn't pay tax. Over time, that compounds significantly.

The Strict Rules (And Why You Need Professional Help)

1031 exchanges have strict IRS rules. If you mess them up, you lose the tax benefit and owe taxes immediately.

Critical rules: * You cannot touch the proceeds. They must go through a qualified intermediary. * You must identify replacement property within 45 days (firm deadline, no extensions). * You must close on replacement property within 180 days. * Both properties must be investment property (not your primary residence different rules apply there). * The replacement property must be equal or greater in value to defer 100% of gains. * You must reinvest all proceeds (including the amount that would've gone to taxes).

This is not a DIY strategy. You need: A qualified intermediary (specialized companies that facilitate 1031 exchanges) * A CPA who understands 1031 rules, A real estate professional experienced with 1031 transactions

But if you're selling investment property and planning to buy more investment property, it's almost always worth exploring.

When 1031 Exchanges Don't Make Sense

You're cashing out of real estate entirely: If you want out of real estate and plan to invest elsewhere, a 1031 doesn't help (you can't exchange into stocks, bonds, or non real estate assets).

You need the cash for something else: If you need proceeds for living expenses, debt payoff, or other non real estate purposes, you can't do a 1031.

The timeline doesn't work: If you can't identify or close on replacement property within the strict deadlines, the exchange fails.

Your gain is small: If your tax liability would only be a few thousand dollars, the cost and complexity of a 1031 might not be worth it.

Capital Gains Tax: What You Need to Know

Even if you're not doing a 1031 exchange, understanding capital gains tax helps you make smarter decisions about when and how to sell.

The Basics

Capital gain = Sale price minus your basis (adjusted cost)
Your basis is typically what you paid for the property, plus major improvements, minus depreciation claimed (for investment properties).

Example: * Purchased property for $150,000, Added $20,000 in improvements (new roof, HVAC) * Adjusted basis: $170,000, Sold for $240,000, Capital gain: $70,000

Tax Rates

Capital gains are taxed differently depending on how long you held the property:

Short term capital gains (held less than 1 year): * Taxed as ordinary income (your normal tax bracket) * Could be 22%, 24%, 32%, or higher depending on your income

Long term capital gains (held more than 1 year): * Taxed at preferential rates: 0%, 15%, or 20% depending on income, Most people pay 15% * High earners may pay 20% * Plus state capital gains tax (varies by state)

Primary residence exclusion: * If you lived in the property as your primary residence for 2 of the last 5 years, you can exclude $250,000 of gains ($500,000 if married filing jointly) * This is huge most people selling their primary home pay zero capital gains tax

Strategies to Minimize Capital Gains Tax

Hold for more than one year: Always try to hold past the 1 year mark to qualify for long term capital gains rates (much lower than short term).

Take advantage of the primary residence exclusion: If you're selling a property you've lived in, make sure you meet the 2 out of 5 year requirement to exclude up to $250k/$500k in gains.

Time the sale strategically: If you're in a high income year, consider waiting until a lower income year to sell (lowers your capital gains tax rate).

Offset gains with losses: If you have investment losses elsewhere (stocks, other properties), you can use them to offset capital gains.

Work with a CPA: Tax planning around property sales can save you thousands. A good CPA will find deductions, credits, and strategies you wouldn't know about.

Selling Directly to Your Tenant

If you're renting out a property and your tenant is interested in buying, selling directly to them can be advantageous.

The Benefits

No marketing or showings: You skip the listing process entirely. No photos, no open houses, no strangers touring the property.

Tenant knows the property: They've lived there. They know the condition. There are fewer surprises during inspection.

Simpler transaction: Both parties are familiar with each other and the property, which can make negotiations smoother.

Motivated buyer: If your tenant wants to stay long term and transition from renting to owning, they're a serious buyer.

How It Works

1. **Gauge interest:** Ask your tenant if they'd be interested in purchasing. If yes, move forward.
2. **Get the property appraised or valued:** You need to know fair market value. Don't just guess or use online estimates.
3. **Negotiate terms:** Price, closing timeline, any repairs or credits.
4. **Involve professionals:** Even though you know the tenant, use real estate professionals or attorneys to handle contracts, title work, and closing properly.
5. **Consider seller financing (if appropriate):** If the tenant has trouble qualifying for traditional financing but you trust them and want monthly income, seller financing might work (you hold the note, they pay you monthly).

When It Makes Sense, Tenant has expressed interest, You're ready to sell and don't want the hassle of marketing, Tenant is financially qualified (or you're comfortable with seller financing)

• Property is in good condition (or tenant accepts it as is)

When to Be Cautious, Tenant has payment issues or conflict history, Property needs significant work and tenant expects you to address it, Price negotiation could damage the landlord tenant relationship if it falls through

Creative Solutions for Distressed Sellers

If you're in financial distress behind on mortgage payments, facing foreclosure, or owing more than the property is worth there are strategies beyond standard sales.

Short Sales

A **short sale** happens when the lender agrees to accept less than the full mortgage balance to allow the property to sell.

Example: * You owe $180,000 on the mortgage, Property is worth $160,000, You're behind on payments and can't afford to continue, The bank agrees to accept $155,000 to release the lien and let the sale proceed

Why lenders agree: They'd rather take $155,000 now than go through foreclosure, which costs them time, money, and often results in a lower recovery.

How it works: * You list the property (usually with an agent experienced in short sales) * When an offer comes in, it's submitted to the lender for approval, The lender reviews financials, hardship documentation, and the offer, If approved, the sale proceeds and the lender forgives the remaining balance

Key points: * Short sales are complex and take time (often 3 6 months) * You need to document financial hardship, Not all lenders approve short sales, Your credit takes a hit (though less than foreclosure) * You may need written authorization for your agent to communicate with the lender

This is why acting early matters. The more time you have before a foreclosure sale date, the better chance a short sale has of succeeding.

Subject To Sales

In a **subject to sale**, the buyer purchases the property and takes over making mortgage payments, but the loan remains in your name.

This is an advanced and risky strategy. It's not common and requires legal expertise. But in certain distressed situations, it can prevent foreclosure and give you an exit.

Why it's risky: * The loan is still in your name (affects your credit and debt to income ratio) * If the buyer stops paying, you're still liable, Most mortgages have a "due on sale" clause that technically allows the lender to call the loan due if ownership transfers

When it's used: Mainly in investor transactions or when a seller is desperate to avoid foreclosure and a traditional sale isn't possible.

Don't attempt this without legal and real estate professional guidance.

Deed in Lieu of Foreclosure

If you can't sell the property and foreclosure is imminent, you can offer the lender a **deed in lieu** you voluntarily transfer ownership back to the bank in exchange for them releasing you from the loan.

Pros: * Avoids formal foreclosure, Faster than foreclosure process, Slightly less damaging to credit than foreclosure

Cons: * You lose the property, Credit still takes a significant hit, Lender may not accept it (especially if there are other liens)

This is a last resort, but it's better than foreclosure if selling isn't possible.

Exit Strategies for Inherited Properties

Inheriting property comes with unique challenges and opportunities. Here's how to navigate them strategically.

Understand the Tax Advantage: Step Up in Basis

When you inherit property, you get a **step up in basis** meaning the property's value for tax purposes is reset to the fair market value on the date of death, not what the deceased owner paid.

Example: * Deceased owner bought property in 1980 for $50,000, Fair market value at death: $250,000, You inherit it with a stepped up basis of $250,000, If you sell it for $250,000 shortly after, you owe zero capital gains tax

This is a huge tax benefit. It's one reason selling inherited property soon after inheriting often makes sense you lock in the step up and avoid future appreciation being taxable.

Dealing With Multiple Heirs

If you're one of several heirs, you have a few options:

Option 1: One heir buys out the others * One person keeps the property and pays the others their share, Clean and simple if one heir wants it and has the funds

Option 2: Sell and split proceeds * List the property, sell it, divide proceeds equally, Most common approach when no heir wants to keep it

Option 3: Rent it and share income * Keep it as a rental and split cashflow, Works if everyone agrees, but can create long term complications

Tip: Get everything in writing. Family conflicts over inherited property are common. Clear agreements prevent disputes.

Probate Considerations

In many states, inherited property goes through probate a legal process where the deceased's assets are distributed according to their will (or state law if there's no will).

Probate can take months or years. During this time, you may not be able to sell without court approval.

Work with a probate attorney to understand your timeline and options. In some cases, you can get court permission to sell before probate fully closes (especially if the property is deteriorating or costing money to maintain).

Timing Strategies: When to Hold, When to Sell

Real estate markets move in cycles. Understanding where your market is can influence when you sell.

Seller's Market vs. Buyer's Market

Seller's market: * Low inventory, high demand, Properties sell quickly, often with multiple offers, Prices rising

Best strategy: If you're ready to sell, do it. You have maximum leverage.

Buyer's market: * High inventory, low demand, Properties sit longer, Prices flat or declining

Best strategy: If you can wait, hold until the market improves. If you need to sell, price aggressively and be realistic about expectations.

Seasonal Considerations

Real estate activity varies by season:

Spring/Summer: Peak selling season, more buyers, higher prices **Fall:** Still active but slowing **Winter:** Slowest season, fewer buyers, but serious ones

If timing allows, list in spring for maximum exposure and competition.

Personal Timing Matters More Than Market Timing

Don't wait for the "perfect" market if your situation demands action. Personal circumstances (financial stress, life changes, health issues) often matter more than waiting for peak market conditions.

Working With the Right Professionals

Advanced strategies require specialized expertise:

CPA or Tax Advisor: Essential for 1031 exchanges, capital gains planning, and tax optimization **Real Estate Attorney:** Important for complex transactions, short sales, probate, and legal issues **Qualified Intermediary:** Required for 1031 exchanges **Experienced Real Estate Agent:** Critical for navigating distressed sales, short sales, and creative solutions

Don't DIY advanced strategies. The cost of professional guidance is almost always less than the cost of mistakes.

When Advanced Strategies Make Sense (And When They Don't)

You Should Explore Advanced Strategies If: You're selling investment property and buying more (1031 exchange)

- You have significant capital gains and want to minimize tax, You're in financial distress and need creative solutions, You're inheriting property with complicated family or legal situations, You have time and resources to navigate complexity

Stick With a Standard Sale If: You're selling your primary residence (primary residence exclusion handles most tax concerns)

- Your capital gains are minimal, You need proceeds quickly and simply, You don't have the capacity or patience for complexity, The cost and effort of advanced strategies outweigh the benefit

The Bottom Line: Protect Your Equity Strategically

Selling property isn't just about getting it off your hands. It's about maximizing what you keep, minimizing what you lose to taxes, and positioning yourself for the best possible outcome.

Sometimes the standard approach is best. List it, sell it, take your proceeds, move on.

But sometimes, taking the time to explore advanced strategies can save you tens of thousands of dollars and create opportunities you wouldn't have otherwise.

The key is knowing which tools exist, when they apply, and having the right professionals to help you execute.

Your equity is too valuable to leave on the table through lack of knowledge or planning.

In the next chapter, we'll pull everything together into a practical toolkit checklists, worksheets, timelines, and resources you can use as you navigate your own property sale.

Let's wrap this up with the tools you need.

15

The Seller's Toolkit

You've read through the strategies, case studies, and guidance. Now it's time to put it all into practice.

This chapter is your practical reference guide the checklists, worksheets, timelines, and key information you'll need as you navigate your property sale. Think of this as your quick reference section that you can return to at each stage of the process.

Keep this chapter bookmarked. Use it as you prepare, list, negotiate, and close your transaction.

Let's get organized.

Pre Sale Decision Checklist

Use this to assess whether selling is the right move for your situation.

Property Assessment * [ ] I know how I acquired this property (purchase, inheritance, divorce, etc.) * [ ] I understand my current equity position (value minus debts) * [ ] I know the property's condition honestly * [ ] I'm aware of any major repairs or deferred maintenance * [ ] I know if there are liens, back taxes, or legal issues

Financial Evaluation * [ ] I've calculated monthly carrying costs (mortgage, taxes, insurance, utilities, maintenance) * [ ] I understand whether the property is cashflow positive or negative * [ ] I know what I'd net from a sale after payoffs and costs * [ ] I've considered opportunity cost (what else could I do with the equity?) * [ ] I understand potential tax implications of selling

Timeline & Urgency * [ ] I know if I'm facing any hard deadlines (foreclosure, reverse mortgage, probate) * [ ] I understand how quickly I need to sell (or if I have flexibility) * [ ] I've evaluated whether I can afford to hold the property longer * [ ] I know if I need proceeds for a specific purpose or timeline

Personal Readiness * [ ] I've assessed my emotional readiness to sell * [ ] I've considered how selling fits my long term goals * [ ] I know where I'll live next (if selling primary residence) * [ ] I've discussed the decision with relevant family members or stakeholders * [ ] I'm clear on what I want to accomplish by selling

If you checked 15+ boxes, you're ready to move forward with selling.

Property Preparation Checklist

Use this before listing your property to ensure it shows well.

Essential Tasks (Do These) * [ ] Deep clean entire property (or hire professional cleaners) * [ ] Declutter all rooms, closets, and storage areas * [ ] Remove excess furniture to make spaces feel larger * [ ] Pack away personal items (photos, collections, personal decor) * [ ] Address peeling paint (interior and exterior) * [ ] Paint scuffed, dirty, or boldly colored walls with neutral colors * [ ] Fix leaky faucets and running toilets * [ ] Replace broken or outdated light fixtures * [ ] Ensure all light bulbs work * [ ] Repair or replace broken cabinet hardware * [ ] Fix doors that don't close properly * [ ] Repair or replace broken window screens * [ ] Ensure all windows open and close * [ ] Tighten loose handrails * [ ] Mow lawn, edge, and trim landscaping * [ ] Add fresh mulch to landscaping beds * [ ] Clean or pressure wash driveway and walkways * [ ] Clean gutters and downspouts * [ ] Remove trash, debris, and clutter from yard * [ ] Test all smoke and CO detectors

Optional (If Budget Allows) * [ ] Professional carpet cleaning (or replacement if heavily stained) * [ ] Update dated light fixtures in kitchen/bathrooms * [ ] Replace old cabinet hardware with modern pulls/knobs * [ ] Paint or replace front door if in poor condition * [ ] Pressure wash exterior siding * [ ] Schedule pre sale home inspection * [ ] Consider professional staging consultation

Don't Waste Money On * [ ] ~~Full kitchen or bathroom renovations~~ * [ ] ~~New flooring throughout (unless destroyed)~~ * [ ] ~~High end upgrades or luxury finishes~~ * [ ] ~~Major landscaping overhauls~~ * [ ] ~~New appliances (unless broken and required)~~

Document Checklist

Gather these documents before meeting with your agent or starting the sale process.

Property Documents * [ ] Deed or title documentation * [ ] Current mortgage statement(s) showing balance and lender info * [ ] Property tax records (current year) * [ ] Homeowners insurance policy and declaration page * [ ] HOA documents (if applicable): bylaws, dues, restrictions * [ ] Survey or plat map (if available) * [ ] Any warranties (roof, HVAC, appliances, etc.)

Disclosure & Compliance * [ ] List of known defects or issues with the property * [ ] Any past inspection reports * [ ] Permits for major work completed (roof, HVAC, electrical, additions) * [ ] Receipts for recent major repairs or improvements * [ ] Any lead paint disclosures (homes built before 1978) * [ ] Well/septic documentation (if applicable)

For Inherited Properties (Additional) * [ ] Death certificate * [ ] Will or trust documents * [ ] Probate court documentation (if applicable) * [ ] Letters of administration or executor appointment * [ ] Contact info for all heirs or beneficiaries

For Investment/Rental Properties (Additional) * [ ] Current lease agreements * [ ] Tenant contact information * [ ] Rent payment history * [ ] Maintenance records * [ ] Property management agreements (if applicable)

Questions to Ask When Interviewing Real Estate Agents

Use these questions to evaluate whether an agent is right for you.

Experience & Expertise * [ ] How long have you been selling real estate? * [ ] How many properties have you sold in the past 12 months? * [ ] Have you worked with properties like mine (distressed, inherited, investment, etc.)? * [ ] Are you familiar with [specific situation: short sales, 1031 exchanges, probate sales, etc.]? * [ ] What's your track record with properties in my price range and neighborhood?

Marketing Strategy * [ ] How will you market my property?

* [ ] What photography and staging services do you provide? * [ ] Where will my listing be advertised? * [ ] How do you handle showings and open houses? * [ ] What sets your marketing apart from other agents?

Pricing & Market Knowledge * [ ] What do you think my property is worth? (Ask for comps to support their answer) * [ ] How did you arrive at that price? * [ ] What's the current market like in my area? * [ ] How long do you expect my property to be on the market? * [ ] What's your strategy if we don't get offers in the first few weeks?

Process & Communication * [ ] What's your typical process from listing to closing? * [ ] How often will you communicate with me? * [ ] How do you handle multiple offers (if we get them)? * [ ] Who will be my main point of contact (you or an assistant)? * [ ] What happens if issues arise during inspection or appraisal?

Commission & Costs * [ ] What's your commission structure? * [ ] What services are included in that commission? * [ ] Are there any upfront costs I should expect? * [ ] Will you offer buyer agent compensation? If so, how much?

References & Results * [ ] Can you provide references from recent sellers? * [ ] Can you share examples of challenging sales you've closed successfully? * [ ] What happens if my property doesn't sell? Do I have flexibility to cancel the listing agreement?

Timeline: Cash Sale to Investor (7 14 Days)

Day 1 2: Initial Contact & Property Assessment * Contact investor or agent with investor network, Schedule property walkthrough, Provide basic info about property condition and situation

Day 2 4: Offer Presentation * Receive cash offer, Review terms, timeline, and conditions, Ask questions, negotiate if needed

Day 5: Accept Offer * Sign purchase agreement, Open escrow/title work begins

Day 6 10: Due Diligence & Title Work * Buyer conducts any final property evaluation (usually minimal for as is sales) * Title company searches title, resolves any issues, Closing documents prepared

Day 11 14: Closing * Final walkthrough (if required) * Sign closing documents, Receive proceeds, Transfer keys and possession

Total Timeline: 7 14 days from first contact to cash in hand

Timeline: Traditional Listing (30 60 Days)

Week 1: Preparation & Launch * Meet with agent, sign listing agreement, Complete property preparation (cleaning, repairs, staging) * Professional photography scheduled and completed, Listing goes live on MLS and syndicates to Zillow, Realtor.com, etc. * Showings begin

Week 2 3: Active Showing Period * Multiple showings scheduled, Open house (if applicable) * Collect feedback from buyer agents, Monitor activity and adjust strategy if needed, Receive offer(s)

Week 3 4: Offer Acceptance & Inspection * Negotiate offer terms, Accept offer, go under contract, Buyer schedules home inspection, Inspection completed, Negotiate any repair requests or credits

Week 4 5: Appraisal & Loan Processing * Buyer's lender

orders appraisal, Appraisal completed, Address any appraisal issues if they arise, Buyer's loan processing continues

Week 5 6: Final Approval & Closing Prep * Loan receives final underwriting approval, Title work completed, Closing date confirmed, Final walkthrough scheduled

Week 6 8: Closing * Final walkthrough conducted, Closing scheduled at title company or attorney's office, Sign documents, transfer title, Receive proceeds, Hand over keys

Total Timeline: 30 60 days from listing to closing

Showing Preparation Checklist

Keep your property show ready with this daily/weekly routine.

Daily (While Listed) * [ ] Make beds and straighten bedrooms * [ ] Clear kitchen counters and sink (dishes washed/put away) * [ ] Wipe down bathroom counters and toilets * [ ] Empty trash cans * [ ] Turn on lights in every room before showings * [ ] Open blinds/curtains to let in natural light * [ ] Adjust temperature to comfortable level (not too hot or cold) * [ ] Contain or remove pets before showings * [ ] Light a subtle candle or use air freshener (not overpowering)

Weekly (While Listed) * [ ] Vacuum all floors and carpets * [ ] Mop hard floors * [ ] Clean bathrooms thoroughly * [ ] Dust surfaces * [ ] Mow lawn and maintain landscaping * [ ] Check for clutter accumulation and remove

Before Each Showing * [ ] Walk through and do a final check * [ ] Turn on all lights * [ ] Make sure property smells fresh (not cooking odors, pet smells) * [ ] Leave the property (buyers feel more comfortable without you there) * [ ] Secure valuables * [ ] Leave contact info for your agent visible if needed

Under Contract Checklist

Track these tasks once you've accepted an offer.

Week 1: Inspection Period * [ ] Provide access for buyer's home inspection * [ ] Receive inspection report * [ ] Negotiate repair requests or credits with buyer * [ ] Complete agreed upon repairs (if any) * [ ] Keep receipts for all work completed

Week 2 3: Appraisal & Loan Processing * [ ] Provide access for appraiser * [ ] Respond to any appraisal issues * [ ] Stay in communication with your agent about buyer's loan progress * [ ] Continue maintaining property

Week 3 4: Final Prep * [ ] Confirm closing date * [ ] Schedule final walkthrough with buyer * [ ] Start packing and preparing to move * [ ] Arrange for utilities to be transferred or shut off after closing * [ ] Forward mail to new address * [ ] Gather all keys, garage remotes, manuals for buyer

Week 4 6: Closing * [ ] Complete final walkthrough with buyer * [ ] Review closing documents before signing * [ ] Bring ID and any required documents to closing * [ ] Sign all paperwork * [ ] Receive proceeds (wire or check) * [ ] Hand over keys, garage remotes, and any other access items * [ ] Confirm property is vacant and clean (if required)

Moving Preparation Timeline

Don't forget about the move itself. Start planning early.

6 8 Weeks Before Closing * [ ] Research moving companies or truck rental options * [ ] Get moving quotes * [ ] Start decluttering and donating items you don't want * [ ] Begin packing non essential items (seasonal items, books, decor)

4 Weeks Before Closing * [ ] Book moving company or

reserve moving truck * [ ] Order packing supplies (boxes, tape, bubble wrap) * [ ] Notify important parties of address change (employer, banks, subscriptions) * [ ] Schedule utility shutoff at old address * [ ] Schedule utility setup at new address

2 Weeks Before Closing * [ ] Pack most belongings (leave only essentials) * [ ] Confirm moving date and details * [ ] Clean out and defrost refrigerator/freezer if taking with you * [ ] Make arrangements for pets and kids on moving day

1 Week Before Closing * [ ] Pack remaining items * [ ] Confirm closing appointment time and location * [ ] Do final walkthrough of property to ensure nothing is missed * [ ] Set aside items you'll need immediately at new place (separate from moving truck)

Closing Day * [ ] Complete final walkthrough with buyer (if scheduled) * [ ] Attend closing, sign documents * [ ] Receive proceeds * [ ] Hand over keys * [ ] Move out and clean property (if not already done)

Key Real Estate Terms (Quick Reference Glossary)

1031 Exchange: A tax deferred exchange allowing you to sell investment property and buy another without paying capital gains tax immediately.

Appraisal: A professional valuation of the property's worth, typically required by lenders.

As Is: Selling the property in its current condition with no repairs or improvements made by the seller.

Capital Gains Tax: Tax owed on the profit from selling an investment property or second home.

Closing: The final step in the sale where documents are signed, money is exchanged, and ownership transfers.

Closing Costs: Fees and expenses paid at closing (title insurance, attorney fees, transfer taxes, etc.).

Comps (Comparable Sales): Recently sold properties similar to yours, used to determine market value.

Contingency: A condition in the purchase agreement that must be met for the sale to proceed (inspection, financing, appraisal).

Days on Market (DOM): The number of days a property has been listed for sale.

Deed: The legal document that transfers property ownership.

Earnest Money: A good faith deposit made by the buyer when submitting an offer.

Equity: The difference between what you owe on the property and its current market value.

Escrow: A neutral third party that holds funds and documents during the transaction.

FSBO (For Sale By Owner): Selling a property without a real estate agent.

Home Inspection: A professional examination of the property's condition, systems, and components.

Listing Agreement: A contract between you and your real estate agent authorizing them to sell your property.

MLS (Multiple Listing Service): A database used by real estate agents to share property listings.

Pre Approval: A letter from a lender stating how much a buyer is qualified to borrow.

Short Sale: Selling a property for less than what's owed on the mortgage, with lender approval.

Title: Legal ownership of the property.

Title Insurance: Insurance that protects against title defects or ownership disputes.

Under Contract: The property has an accepted offer and is in the process of closing.

Resources and Professional Contacts

Who You Might Need

Real Estate Agent/Broker: * Handles listing, marketing, showings, negotiations, and transaction coordination, When to use: For most traditional sales, investment properties, or complex situations

Real Estate Attorney: * Handles legal aspects, contract review, title issues, probate, When to use: Complex transactions, legal disputes, inherited properties, or states where attorneys are required for closings

CPA/Tax Advisor: * Handles tax planning, capital gains strategies, 1031 exchange guidance, When to use: Investment property sales, large capital gains, 1031 exchanges, inherited properties

Home Inspector: * Conducts pre sale or buyer inspections, When to use: Pre sale inspections to identify issues before listing

Appraiser: * Provides professional property valuation, When to use: When you need accurate market value (not just online estimates)

Title Company: * Handles title search, title insurance, and closing, When to use: Every sale (typically arranged by your agent or attorney)

Qualified Intermediary: * Facilitates 1031 exchanges, When to use: Any 1031 exchange transaction

Estate/Probate Attorney: * Handles inherited property legal issues, When to use: Probate sales, estate planning, multiple heirs, complex inheritance situations

Contractor/Handyman: * Handles repairs and improvements, When to use: Pre sale repairs, addressing inspection items

Final Checklist: Are You Ready to Sell?

Before you list, confirm: * [ ] I've decided selling is the right move for my situation * [ ] I understand my options (cash sale vs. listing) * [ ] I've chosen the right real estate professional to work with * [ ] My property is prepared and shows well * [ ] I have realistic pricing expectations based on comps and condition * [ ] I have all necessary documents gathered * [ ] I understand the timeline and process * [ ] I know where I'm going next (housing or proceeds plan) * [ ] I'm ready to be responsive and engaged throughout the process

If you've checked all boxes, you're ready to move forward.

How to Use This Toolkit

Keep this chapter as your reference guide throughout the selling process:

When deciding whether to sell: Use the Pre Sale Decision Checklist **When preparing to list:** Use the Property Preparation Checklist and Document Checklist **When choosing an agent:** Use the Questions to Ask **When tracking the process:** Use the appropriate Timeline (Cash or Traditional) **When managing showings:** Use the Showing Preparation Checklist **When under contract:** Use the Under Contract Checklist **When planning your move:** Use the Moving Preparation Timeline **When you need definitions:** Reference the Key Terms Glossary

This toolkit gives you structure, clarity, and confidence as you navigate your sale.

You've got this.

In the final chapter, we'll bring everything together with some closing thoughts on making this transition successfully and making your next move your best move.

16

Final Words: Clarity, Confidence, Control

You've reached the end of this book, but hopefully the beginning of something better a clearer path forward, a stronger sense of what's possible, and the confidence to make decisions that serve your actual goals instead of avoiding the ones that scare you.

When you started reading, you might have been overwhelmed, stuck, or unsure of what to do with a property that wasn't serving you anymore. Maybe you were stressed about a foreclosure timeline, confused about an inheritance, frustrated by tenants you couldn't manage, or simply ready to move on from a house that no longer fit your life.

Whatever brought you here, you now have something you didn't have before: **information.**

And information changes everything.

What You Now Have: Clarity

You understand the signs that indicate it's time to sell not just the obvious financial signals, but the emotional, legal, and practical ones too. You know how to assess whether a property is truly an asset or a burden dressed as one.

You know your options: cash sale for speed and certainty, listing for maximum value, or holding strategically if that serves your goals. You understand the trade offs of each path and can evaluate which one fits your situation.

You understand how the process actually works from preparing the property and pricing it realistically, to navigating inspections, appraisals, and the under contract period. You're not walking into this blind.

You've seen real stories of real people who faced tough decisions and found paths forward. You've learned from their successes and their challenges.

You have clarity and that's the foundation of good decision making.

What You Now Have: Confidence

You know what professional real estate help actually looks like and why it matters. You understand the difference between working with a cash investor network and listing on the open market. You know why FSBO often backfires and what you're giving up when you try to save a commission.

You understand pre sale inspections, strategic repairs, and how to prepare a property without overspending. You know about 1031 exchanges, capital gains tax, and advanced strategies that can protect your equity.

You've seen the timelines, the checklists, the questions to ask, and the terms you need to know.

You're not an expert but you're informed. And that's enough to make smart decisions and hold your own in conversations with professionals.

What You Now Have: Control

This might be the most important shift of all.

When you don't understand your options, you feel stuck. You feel like things are happening *to* you instead of decisions you're making *for* yourself.

But now you know: You can sell quickly if you need to, You can maximize value if you have time, You can protect equity through strategic planning, You can navigate complexity with the right guidance, You can make this transition successfully

You're not trapped. You have agency. You have control over what happens next.

And that changes how you approach this decision not from a place of fear or desperation, but from a place of strategy and intentionality.

The Decision Is Yours

We've given you information, frameworks, and tools. We've shown you what's possible and what to watch out for.

But we haven't told you what to do.

Because that's not our job. **The decision is yours.**

Only you know: What you're trying to accomplish, What your timeline looks like, What your risk tolerance is, What's keeping you up at night, What would make your life better

Our job the job of this book was to give you the knowledge and confidence to make that decision well.

If you're ready to sell, you know how to do it strategically.

If you're not ready yet, you know what signs to watch for and when to revisit the decision.

If you're somewhere in between, you know what questions to ask and who to talk to.

There's no pressure here. Just information and options.

Making Your Next Move Your Best Move

This phrase has appeared throughout the book, and it's not just a tagline. It's a philosophy.

Selling a property isn't just about getting rid of something you don't want. It's about creating space financial, emotional, logistical for something better.

Tiffany Wills sold her failed renovation project and bought a home that actually fit her life. She didn't just escape a problem she moved toward a solution.

The condo owner sold an underperforming rental and doubled their cashflow by repositioning into a better investment. They didn't just liquidate they leveled up.

The heirs who almost lost their inherited property to a tax sale walked away with money that bought cars, secured housing, and stabilized their lives. They didn't just avoid disaster they created opportunity.

The burned out landlord escaped chaos and reinvested into peace of mind. He didn't just quit he upgraded his quality of life.

The aging homeowner sold the stairs that were endangering her and moved into independence and community. She didn't just adapt she thrived.

Every one of these sellers made their next move their best move because they approached the decision with clarity, strategy, and help from people who knew how to navigate the complexity.

That's what we want for you.

Not just a closed transaction, but a better situation on the other side.

You Don't Have to Do This Alone

One of the biggest messages in this book is this: **selling property especially complicated property benefits from professional guidance.**

That's not about us trying to sell you on hiring someone. It's about recognizing reality.

You can learn to cut your own hair, fix your own car, or represent yourself in court. People do it. Some even succeed.

But when the outcome really matters when you're navigating complexity, when the stakes are high, when one mistake could cost you thousands most people choose to work with someone who does this every day.

Real estate professionals exist for a reason. Not because you're incapable, but because experience, systems, and specialized knowledge deliver better outcomes than DIY trial and error.

The right professional doesn't take control away from you they give you more control by handling the details you don't have time or expertise for, spotting problems before they become disasters, and negotiating on your behalf.

You're still making the decisions. They're just making sure

those decisions are informed, protected, and executed well.

One Last Thought: The Property Doesn't Define You

If you're feeling guilty, ashamed, or frustrated about the situation you're in with your property, let that go.

Owning a property you can't manage, don't want, or can't afford doesn't make you a failure.

Life happens. Relationships end. People get sick. Jobs are lost. Markets shift. Plans change. Inheritances come with complications you didn't choose.

You're not the first person to face this. You won't be the last. And the fact that you're reading this book seeking information, exploring options, trying to make the best decision you can says everything about your character.

The property doesn't define you. What defines you is how you handle the situation.

And right now, you're handling it by educating yourself, thinking strategically, and preparing to take action.

That's something to be proud of.

An Invitation

If you're ready to explore your options whether that's a cash offer, listing your property, or just having a conversation about what makes sense for your situation we'd be honored to help.

We work with sellers every day who are facing exactly what you're facing. Distressed properties. Inherited homes. Rental nightmares. Foreclosure timelines. Properties that just don't fit anymore.

We're not here to pressure you or push you into a decision

you're not ready for. We're here to help you understand your specific situation, explore your options, and make the move that serves your goals.

If you want to talk, reach out.

No obligation. No hard sell. Just honest conversation about what's possible and what makes sense for you.

You can contact us at:

DLTA, Direct Lead To Action Phone: (312) 561 7484

Or, if you're not ready to reach out yet, that's okay too. Keep this book. Reference it when you need it. Share it with someone else who might be in a similar situation.

The information here doesn't expire. It'll be here when you're ready.

Your Next Move Starts Now

Selling a property especially one that's been causing you stress, costing you money, or trapping equity you need is one of the most significant financial decisions you'll make.

But it's also one of the most liberating.

On the other side of this transaction is freedom.

Freedom from: Monthly payments you can't sustain, Repairs you can't afford, Tenants you can't manage, A property that doesn't serve your goals anymore

And freedom to: Move into housing that actually fits your life, Invest equity into something that performs better, Pay off debt and reduce financial stress, Build the future you want instead of being anchored to the past

That's what this decision makes possible.

You've spent time with this book. You've absorbed the information. You've seen the case studies. You've reviewed the checklists and timelines.

Now it's time to act.

Not impulsively. Not out of fear. But intentionally, strategically, and with the confidence that comes from knowing what you're doing.

Your property situation doesn't have to stay the way it is. You're not stuck. You have options. You have information. You have a path forward.

All that's left is to take the first step.

And we're here to walk it with you.

Closing Thought

Real estate is just property walls, floors, roofs. But the decisions you make about property shape your life in profound ways.

They determine where you live, how you spend your money, what opportunities you can pursue, and how much stress you carry every day.

Making good real estate decisions isn't about being the smartest person in the room. It's about being informed, strategic, and willing to act when the time is right.

You have everything you need to make this decision well.

Clarity. Confidence. Control.

Now go make your next move your best move.

We're rooting for you.

** Tom and the Team at DLTA**

When It's Time to Sell A House Money Press Publication